Marinus Willett

Historian Benson J. Lossing included this view of Fort Ontario in his 1860 *Pictorial Field-Book of the Revolution*. Supposedly it is based on a 1798 woodcut and represents the closest known approximation of the fort's appearance at the time of Willett's attempt to seize it.

MARINUS WILLETT

Defender of the Northern Frontier

by Larry Lowenthal

PURPLE MOUNTAIN PRESS
Fleischmanns, New York

Marinus Willett: Defender of the Northern Frontier

First edition 2000

Published by
PURPLE MOUNTAIN PRESS, LTD.
P.O. Box 309, Fleischmanns, New York 12430-0309
914-254-4062, 914-254-4476 (fax), purple@catskill.net
http://www.catskill.net/purple

Library of Congress Cataloging-in-Publication Data

Lowenthal, Larry.
    Marinus Willett : defender of the northern frontier / by Larry Lowenthal.-- 1st ed.
    p. cm. -- (New Yorkers and the Revolution)
    Includes bibliographical references (p.) and index.
    ISBN 1-930098-07-3 (pbk. : alk. paper)
    1. Willett, Marinus, 1740-1830. 2. United States--History--Revolution,
1775-1783--Campaigns. 3. New York (State)--History--Revolution, 1775-1783. 4.
Soldiers--New York (State)--Biography. I. Title. II. Series.

E207.W65 L68 2000
973.3'3--dc21
                                                                    00-032352

Manufactured in the United States of America on acid-free paper.

Table of Contents

To commemorate the gallant and patriotic act of Marinus Willett in here seizing, June 6th, 1775, from British forces the muskets with which he armed his troops, this tablet is erected by the Society of the Sons of the Revolution, New York, Nov, 1892.

INTRODUCTION

IN THE DIMLY LIGHTED ENTRYWAY of an office building only a few doors away from the nerve center of international capitalism in lower Manhattan hangs a plaque which commemorates an event that took place in a much different world. Originally dedicated and mounted in 1892, it recalls a human-scaled New York of solid, dormered houses, thickets of masts along the waterfront and a society built around personal contact. Greenwich Village and today's Lower East Side lay out in a pleasant countryside of orchards and ponds.

But the impression given by the secure domesticity of the houses and lively prosperity of the streets was deceptive, for the city was being torn apart by fierce political disputes, conflicts all the more acute because the rivals were too well acquainted with each other. By the date commemorated on the plaque, June 6, 1775, though only a few would have dared to express such ideas, British rule was coming to an end.

The events of June 6 were part of the troubled childbirth of a new nation. On that day one man stepped forward to challenge royal authority. He may have had a few supporters with him, and in an hour he could have mobilized hundreds of Sons of Liberty, but at that moment he was alone—one man defying the British Empire when that empire stood unchallenged at the peak of its power.

The man who stood up that day was Marinus Willett. At that moment he symbolized the colonists' determination to protect what they considered their just rights and warned the royal government how difficult it would be to suppress those aspirations. This was the first time Marinus Willett won the attention and admiration of the people. The audacity he displayed that day would be repeated many times over as he became the hero of Fort Stanwix and the Mohawk Valley.

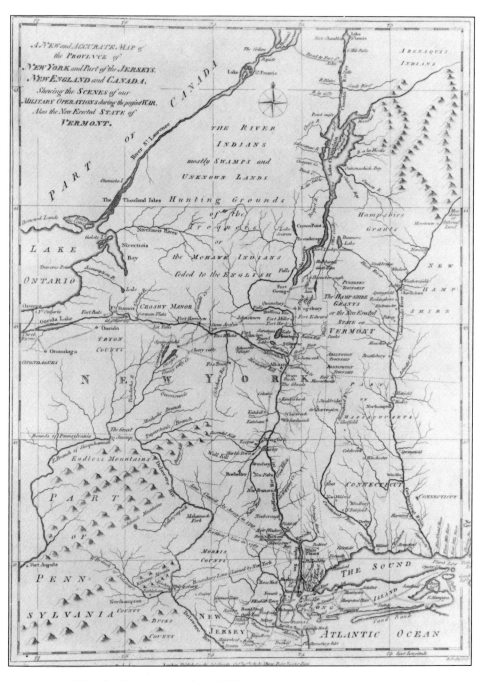

Map by J. Bew, London, 1780. Courtesy New York State Museum

I. A TRUE SON OF LIBERTY

THE SONS OF LIBERTY arose as a direct consequence of the British government's attempt to impose a stamp tax on the colonies in 1765. In New York this crisis radicalized a political scene already seething with factionalism. Though few Sons of Liberty would have dared utter the word independence in their most private thoughts, the events they set in motion led to that result, as surely as one tiny leak in an earthen dam will eventually wash away the entire structure.

When the Stamp Act crisis exploded, Marinus Willett was 25 years old, a native New Yorker and already a war veteran. Active, intense, a young man of quick passions, he was bound to be affected by the tumult around him. He became and remained a true Son of Liberty, dedicated to their goals even when the organization itself faded, and guided by their principles long after independence had been won.

Yet in some ways Willett seemed an unlikely choice to rebel against royal authority. He had volunteered to serve in the British Army, and his father was a devout believer in rule by the king and Church of England. It was a solid, long-established family, which on occasion had achieved a degree of prominence. Marinus's grandfather and great-grandfather had been county sheriffs on Long Island, and the great-grandfather held the rank of colonel in the militia.

Marinus Willett was born July 31, 1740, in Jamaica, New York. Now the end of subway lines, Jamaica then was a farming and trading village far out on Long Island. Marinus was named for a great uncle, Marinus Van Varick. As the name indicates, he represented the blending of English and Dutch heritage that made New York (and neighboring northern New Jersey) distinctive among the colonies.

Years later, after the United States had won its independence, an embittered New York Loyalist, Thomas Jones, wrote his version of the conflict. He was acquainted with the Willetts, to whom he was related by marriage, and described them as "a good family, but which by misfortunes . . . had been for many years reduced."[1] Though Jones shunned giving the rebels credit if he could avoid it, this depiction is probably accurate. One reason for the strained circumstances may be that there were 13 children, of which Marinus was the tenth and the last son. One child had died by the time Marinus was born, and three others were lost before he was ten. They died not in infancy, but in the full promise of youth, so an air of tragedy must have pervaded the household and tested the firm faith of the parents.

No incidents of Marinus's childhood survive. It must have been a typical rural boyhood in a pleasant countryside, occasionally salted by breezes from the sea. His father, Edward (1702-1794) was a school teacher sponsored by the Society for Propagating the Gospel, so Marinus must have received a decent education in the parish school, as his later letters show. When Marinus was a boy his father secured the privilege of operating a ferry between New York and Long Island. He apparently gave this up after a few years, for around 1749 he crossed over to Manhattan and began a 25-year career as a tavern operator.

It seems odd for a somewhat rustic and deeply religious man to make a career running a tavern in what was already a diverse and sophisticated town. Nevertheless, Edward Willett apparently succeeded. The most famous of the several taverns he ran was the Province Arms, located on Broadway near Trinity Church, with a striking view down to the Hudson and the steep Palisades on the New Jersey side. The tavern was the former residence of James DeLancey, leader of a conservative faction in New York politics, who had vacated it to build a mansion in the country near the Lower East Side street that now bears his name. Edward Willett's clients were mostly well-to-do and reinforced his deeply orthodox religious and political beliefs. For young Marinus it must have been an unexcelled education to observe the variety of people who frequented the Province Arms and the bustling nearby streets: pompous office-holders brushing against rowdy sailors and energetic tradesmen.

Much of what we know of Marinus Willett's life comes to us from a book produced by his son a year after his death. Entitled *A Narrative of the Military Actions of Colonel Marinus Willett*, it is based on a manuscript prepared by the Colonel late in his life.[2] But Willett did not describe his entire career; furthermore, there is reason to suspect that his son, with the sensibilities of a different generation, may have expurgated portions that made him uncomfortable.

In this book the only incident of Willett's youth that is recorded is his observation of a British press-gang at work on the streets of New York in 1756. Another war with France was raging, the fourth since 1689. Fought primarily over European issues, with West Indies islands as a secondary prize, these conflicts invariably spilled over into North America. Seeking crews to man its warships, a party of British marines went ashore to impress sailors on the city streets. As Willett described it, "They commenced their business very early in the morning; and though it was afterwards said that their orders were to impress only such as had the appearance of seafaring or labouring men, yet several respectable citizens were seized by those press-gangs, who scrupled not to enter into whatsoever house they pleased, without regarding the terror or protestations of the occupants."[3]

Featured prominently in the *Narrative*, this incident is clearly meant to be seen as a defining event in young Willett's life, the source of his subsequent hatred of royal authority. It is all the more surprising, then, to find Willett joining the British Army less than two years later. The North American phase of the struggle had been going badly for England. In 1755 Gen. James Braddock's army had been nearly annihilated in an attempt to take Fort Duquesne (now Pittsburgh). Two years later a British garrison was forced to surrender Fort William Henry, at the southern end of Lake George, to French General Montcalm. After the battle, Montcalm was unable to restrain the Indians who made up a large part of his force, and many British captives were robbed and murdered.

Now in 1758 a new surge of patriotism and excitement gripped the northern colonies. New armies were put in motion, and in their ranks was Marinus Willett, not yet 18 years old, but holding a commission as second lieutenant in a New York regiment. The commander of the regiment was Oliver DeLancey, brother of the lieutenant governor of the colony. Willett had obtained his commission through family influence, and the fact that colonial leaders passed their time at the Province Arms did no harm. Willett, always conscious of his appearance, later described his first uniform: "a green coat, trimmed with silver twist, white under clothes and black gaiters; also a cocked hat, with a large cockade of silk ribbon, together with a silver button and loop."[4]

Thus resplendently attired, Willett sailed upriver to Albany and was immediately sent west into the Mohawk Valley to protect its settlements against French and Indian incursions. Quickly the glamour of military life gave way to a harsher reality. Slogging over sandy roads to Schenectady on a warm May day, Willett remembered this first march as the most fatiguing he ever made. Many others lay ahead.

Soon afterward, DeLancey's regiment was ordered northward to join a great army assembling at Lake George with the goal of capturing Fort Carillon (now Ticonderoga) and driving the French off Lake Champlain. Although the nominal commander of the British army was Brig. Gen. James Abercromby, its spirit resided in Lord George Howe. This remarkable young nobleman, deservedly popular even among the colonial troops, seemed to be a model for a new kind of British officer, freed from stifling traditions and open to new methods of fighting in the wilderness.

On June 5, 1758, the British army sailed down Lake George in a display of pageantry and strength such as had never been seen in North America. A day later they landed at the north end of the lake, near Ticonderoga, with little opposition. Here Willett saw Indians who were with Abercromby's army bring in two fresh scalps of French soldiers.[5] This made a powerful impression on the young lieutenant, a 17-year-old city boy.

Willett long remembered his feelings as he anticipated his first battle. "Neither at this time, nor upon any subsequent occasion, did he experience the least degree of fear. On the contrary, he uniformly found his spirits elated, as the crisis approached. . . . Now, when expecting every instant to come in contact with the enemy, though young and unacquainted with danger, his spirits were highly exhilarated."[6]

Lord Howe, who represented so much of the hope of the British army, was killed in an almost accidental encounter. A large part of the formidable army seemed to dissolve in chaos. Abercromby, who apparently had not expected to lead troops in the field, was befuddled. Although this luckless commander was only 52, contemporaries described him in terms normally used for the decrepit.

On the next day the army regrouped and resumed its march toward the French fortress. Willett's unit blundered into the defending force, protected behind abatis (felled trees and brush), and Willett was lucky to escape a blast of enemy fire. From this point he had a full view of the main battle, as Abercromby launched a series of infantry assaults against entrenched French positions on the approaches to the fort. Picked British troops attacked with superb discipline and were piled up in heaps against the French breastworks.

Exhausted, Willett and his companions fell into a deep sleep, expecting the attack to be resumed the next day. Instead, the British army made a disorganized and humiliating retreat. Abercromby, despite having wasted 2000 men, still outnumbered the French by more than three to one. Nor had he used his powerful artillery, with which he could have driven the French from their outworks and probably battered an entry into the fort. It had been one of the most disgraceful days in British military history, and through no fault of the common soldier.

Eager to salvage something from the disaster, Abercromby authorized an attack on another French fort, Frontenac, located at the point where the St. Lawrence opens into Lake Ontario. Command was given to American Col. John Bradstreet, who had been promoting the idea for several years. His detachment was part of a larger expedition commanded by Brig. Gen. John Stanwix, who was directed to construct a major fort at the Oneida Carrying Place. This was a strategic portage across a low divide in central New York where the Mohawk River, flowing into the Hudson, came within a couple of miles of Wood Creek, which led to Lake Ontario.

Bradstreet, who in vigor and initiative was the polar opposite of Abercromby, led a force of 3000. Included were DeLancey's New Yorkers, Willett among them. Moving with maximum haste to avoid detection by the French, Bradstreet left the Oneida Carry on August 15, reached Oswego on August 21, and six days later had captured Fort Frontenac and its garrison. The return journey, far from being a triumphant march, proved to be a terrible ordeal. Fearing French retaliation, Bradstreet drove his men to and beyond their limits. Men already wearied by forced marching exhausted themselves pushing batteaux (or battoes: flat-bottomed boats propelled by wind or poles and commonly used on the shallow waterways of central New York) loaded with captured loot against the current. In his final report General Stanwix wrote that "This Enterprize was performed with so much expedition & fatigue that few could bear it."[7]

Only one man had been lost taking Fort Frontenac, but hundreds died on the return. Lieutenant Willett, not yet fully mature, was tough enough to survive, but barely. On his arrival at Fort Stanwix, as the new work at the Carry was named, he became desperately ill. He lingered in camp until he had recovered enough to attempt the trip home, which he finally reached on December 7, 1758. The return of this casualty must have been doubly welcome to the Willett family, for news had been received that Marinus's brother Isaac, eight years older, had been lost at sea while serving on a British privateer.

In the next two years British arms redeemed themselves; commanded by energetic leaders, they took Quebec and Montreal, driving the French from Canada and the Great Lakes. Marinus Willett took no part in this; still in a weakened state, his first episode of soldiering had come to an end.

As a youngster during the French and Indian War, Willett performed creditably despite his complete inexperience. The war was important in his life not for what he contributed to British victory, but for the lessons he learned. It is unlikely that he had previously seen the frontiers of New York or had contact with Indians. Willett had received no formal military training and did not come from one of those hereditary military families in which warfare and its traditions are discussed around the dinner table. His military academy was conducted under the walls of Forts Carillon and Frontenac.

Several other young officers who were later prominent in the War for Independence—George Clinton, James Clinton and Philip Schuyler among them—received a similar education. They learned at close range the strength and weakness of the British army. Among the high officers were men of courage and ability and others who were hopeless incompetents. The British soldiers were unafraid to die; their lives were often squandered by their officers; but they were hardly invincible. More important, Willett came back unconvinced that colonial troops were inevitably inferior to regulars.

Military laurels soon wither. Marinus Willett was approaching 19 years of age as his physical vigor began to return; he needed to find a career. Although a standard biographical dictionary claims that he graduated Columbia (then Kings) College, this is almost certainly an error.[8] He was suited neither temperamentally nor financially for college. If he hadn't attended before his military service, he was rather old by the standards of the time to begin afterwards; besides, he soon married.

This period is largely a blank in the record of Willett's life. Many years later a son claimed not to know how Marinus had earned a living before the War for Independence.[9] Tradition states that he worked as a cabinetmaker, and that seems reasonable enough. The tradition further asserts that he married his employer's daughter, Mary Pearsee. They were married April 2, 1760, and a son, Marinus, was born in 1762.

In normal times Marinus Willett's destiny would have been that of a nameless "mechanic" as his class was called, perhaps chronically angry at the lack of an outlet for his restless energy. Instead, it was his fate to live in an age of tumult, a time of upheaval that created opportunities usually not available to a young man in his station.

Willett's true calling was that of a rebel. He never wavered in his dedication to the struggle for liberty or his willingness to take risks to achieve it. Indeed, the depth of his commitment is difficult to explain. It is hard to see how one or several incidents of British arrogance, such as the action of the press gang, could have had such a profound impact. His father and most of the family were devout loyalists. Cases of sons rebelling against fathers are hardly unusual. This may be a factor—without knowing more about the interaction of that family, one cannot be sure—but even this explanation seems inadequate to account for Willett's exceptional fervor. Jones, ever caustic, says that "When the troubles began, he thought, as many others did, that by opposing Great Britain, and taking an active part on the side of the rebellion, something might be gotten, at all events nothing could be lost."[10] True, as Jones portrays him, Willett "was never worth a farthing," but again, it is difficult to attribute his zeal to mere opportunism.[11]

What Jones calls the "troubles" was not a continuous crisis, but rather a series of alarms interrupted by periods of quiet when it looked as though it might be possible to preserve royal government. At each crisis Willett was one of the radicals who, like reverse firemen, dashed out to fan the flames. Protests against the Stamp Act turned violent. On October 31, 1764, a mob surged out of control and burned an effigy of Lieutenant Governor Colden, as well as some of his property. Some went on to ransack the home of a British major who had threatened to ram the stamps down American throats at sword point.

Repeal of the Stamp Act brought a few years of quiet. The Sons
of Liberty, while perhaps no longer maintaining a regular organization, awaited another occasion. Once again British bungling insensi-
tivity gave them one. During disturbances stemming from
enforcement of the unpopular Quartering Acts, which required
colonists to house British soldiers in their homes, redcoats tore down
a liberty pole and threw a prominent agitator into jail. A brawl broke
out between rioters and a detachment of soldiers on January 19, 1770.
Known as the Battle of Golden Hill, this was New York's equivalent
of the Boston Massacre, which took place several weeks later. The
difference was that in this case the soldiers did not fire; though they
used swords and bayonets, the rioters fought back, and eventually
the soldiers retired to their barracks.

Boston and New York continued to move in tandem: Boston had
a tea party December 16, 1773. Paul Revere brought news of this
event to New York on December 21, and that town staged its own
version April 22, 1774. In the interval between these festivities,
Parliament passed what American agitators called the "Intolerable
Acts." From that moment on the crisis became continuous, flowing
in an uninterrupted sweep to Lexington, Bunker Hill and July 4,
1776. In Manhattan, Marinus Willett was at the center of events that
marked the effective end of colonial rule, except when enforced under
the bayonets of British garrisons.

During the disintegration of colonial government, New York
City was controlled by three successive committees, each with a more
radical composition than its predecessor. It is revealing that Willett,
despite his prominence, was not a member of any of these governing
bodies. The Sons of Liberty was founded and managed by relatively
well-to-do lawyers and businessmen such as John Morin Scott. Below
them was a layer of mechanics and tradesmen, of which Willett was
representative. Another step lower was an unruly mass of sailors and
laborers, always on the verge of becoming a mob.[12]

It is clear that Willett's main participation was as a rabble-rouser
and street brawler—duties for which his size, fearlessness, articulate-
ness and zeal made him uniquely valuable. We tend to forget that a
good deal of the dominance achieved by the "patriot" party was due
to physical intimidation, not to its more cogent interpretations of
Locke and Montesquieu. This is why later historians and members
of honorific organizations—as well as Marinus Willett's son, for that

matter—have had difficulty integrating the Sons of Liberty or the victims of the Boston Massacre into their revolutionary pantheon. Only a few of Willett's exploits in the Sons of Liberty have been sketchily recorded. His talents were not those of the council chamber or the study; thoroughly a man of action, his abilities were in the streets, where his ardor could inspire and direct the mob.

It was Willett's special contribution to see early that war was coming and to prepare for it. Weapons were essential, and in the beginning, at least, the rebels would have to fight with captured arms. On April 23, 1775, a dusty messenger galloped down the post road to New York, bringing news as thunderous as his horse's hooves: patriot blood had been shed at Lexington and Concord. Almost immediately Willett and his associates responded by seizing the arsenal and confiscating the weapons stored there.

On June 6 occurred the incident for which Willett became most famous. It is the only one mentioned in the *Narrative*, perhaps because it is the only one that could be considered at all "military." The small British garrison remaining in New York had been given permission to depart for Boston. Willett personally thought this was a mistake, as the soldiers could easily have been disarmed and taken prisoner; the committee governing the city was not ready for such extreme action. The departing troops were allowed to take their personal arms and equipment. Willett was in a tavern "in company with a half dozen more of the same sentiments and spirit as himself," when word came that the British were carrying away cartloads of arms.

The group dashed off to spread the word. Willett was coming down Broad Street when he saw the British carts approaching, accompanied by a small guard. On impulse, but with typical audacity, he dashed forward and stopped the lead horse. The British major commanding the detachment blustered up to demand what was happening. The soldiers were not authorized to carry off spare arms, Willett replied boldly. Attracted by the commotion, the mayor appeared and inquired why Willett was risking a disturbance. The mayor was regarded as a zealous Tory, and Willett replied that "considering the bloody business which had taken place among our brethren in Massachusetts . . . he deemed it his duty to prevent these arms from being used against them."[13]

Next, Gouverneur Morris came up. He was a respected patriot, but a cautious one, and he staggered Willett by agreeing with the mayor. Willett's prospects were looking grim, but at that moment lawyer John Morin Scott appeared. Scott was one of the intellectual founders of the Sons of Liberty, and his word carried great weight. After listening to explanations, he supported Willett. Furthermore, he suggested that Willett address the troops. This was like throwing fresh meat to a hungry lion; Willett leaped up on one of the carts and began haranguing the troops. If you don't care to shed the blood of your countrymen, come over to the side of freedom, he shouted. So persuasive was Willett that one soldier risked execution by heeding the American's call. He and five carts of arms were led up Broadway; the other British soldiers, with only their personal weapons, marched down to the wharf. On a brilliant June morning, one man had successfully defied the British Empire.

Willett made a third, more obscure, stroke aimed at seizing British arms. On July 20, 1775, he and a few other resolute Sons of Liberty procured a sloop at Greenwich, Connecticut, sailed it through the treacherous waters of Hell Gate (where the Harlem and East Rivers meet Long Island Sound) and at midnight surprised the guard and captured a British storehouse at Turtle Bay. This was a secluded cove, surrounded by steep banks, on the east shore of Manhattan; today it is the location of the United Nations. Willett had again shown his aptitude for the daring, decisive strike.

II. THE HERO OF FORT STANWIX

*To search for information where the enemy were vulnerable and endeav-
our to procure permission to assault 'em there . . . was a doctrine I took
no small pains to inculcate, from a conviction of the importance of
incouraging a spirit of enterprise in a young and new-formed army. . . .
I have made it my regular business to seek for opportunities of meeting
my enemies in the field.* —Marinus Willett, April 1, 1781.[14]

A N UNDERAPPRECIATED ASPECT of winning independence was
the ability of the rebels to establish governments. In New York
this was accomplished despite all the advantages of continuity, experience, money, and control of the legal apparatus that the loyalists
enjoyed. For a brief period two administrations functioned uneasily
side-by-side, but the rebel government prevailed. Tory administration could not thrive beyond the reach of British bayonets, whereas
the patriot government survived defeat, pursuit, and financial col-
lapse.

Showing its determination early in its existence, the rebel government of New York created a military force out of little more than
enthusiasm. Tories sneered that the rebels who yelled the loudest in
the taverns and street-corners would be the most allergic to gunpow-
der, but that was not the case with the leading Sons of Liberty, and
certainly was not true of Marinus Willett. New York organized four
regiments, one of which was commanded by Alexander McDougall,
a conspicuous Son of Liberty. On June 28, 1775, Marinus Willett
accepted a commission as captain in this regiment. These troops were
armed largely with weapons that had been seized in his exploits.

Only six weeks later, Willett and his company sailed up the
Hudson, as the youthful Marinus had done 17 years before. Their
destination was Canada, which the Continental Congress had deter-

mined to conquer. This invasion, made possible when Ethan Allen and Benedict Arnold captured Fort Ticonderoga on May 10, 1775, made strategic sense. Most Canadians were thought to sympathize with the American revolt; furthermore, capturing the 14th colony would deprive the British of a base from which they could attack the northern colonies.

Unfortunately, while Congress was advanced enough to send armies northward, organizing and supplying these forces was beyond its ability. Pushing toward Montreal the Americans were stalled by a British fort at St. Johns (St. Jean). Although St. Johns, with much of the meager British garrison in Canada, fell on November 2, the delay meant a winter campaign against Quebec. An attack on that fortress by freezing, starving American troops failed on the last day of 1775.

Willett, whose main qualifications were "his health, his strength, the buoyancy of his spirits, his enthusiasm," as the *Narrative* put it, made a good reputation in the Canada campaign. After escorting prisoners back to Ticonderoga, he was placed in command at St. Johns. The American army, full of men whose concept of liberty did not embrace military discipline, was ravaged by insubordination. Willett's conduct—level-headed, dedicated and efficient—rose above this morass and impressed Gen. Philip Schuyler, commander of the Northern Department. Willett was receptive to the new experiences he encountered. In a letter to his son he described the buildings and religious ceremonies of Montreal, "somewhat Farcical & some very solemn. . . ."[15]

In January 1776 the enlistments of Willett's men expired, and they headed home. Willett performed some further duties as sort of a knight errant, then returned to New York in March. Although he had seen combat in the early fighting around St. Johns, he must have chafed at the fact that so much of his later time was occupied with garrison and escort duties. Not only had he earned little glory, but the performance of the raw American troops convinced him that the country faced a long and grinding war.

Worse was to come. Willett missed the tragic conclusion of the Canadian campaign, when the army that had surged forth so bravely stumbled out of Canada ruined by disease, demoralization and indiscipline. The disaster was all the more poignant because many of the soldiers—like Willett enlisting at the outset of the war—were true idealists, committed to the revolutionary cause. Their ardor was squandered in squalid camps around Lake Champlain, where these promising men died miserably and anonymously of smallpox, bowel complaints and hunger.

In New York City Willett participated in the next American disaster. The British had been forced to evacuate Boston, but in July 1776 Sir William Howe, a younger brother of Lord George Howe who had been killed at Ticonderoga, arrived in New York Bay on a fleet commanded by another brother, Lord Richard. In battles around New York City, General Howe repeatedly outmaneuvered Washington but just as often let slip opportunities to destroy the American army. Meanwhile, Marinus Willett had lost a captaincy in the new Fourth New York Regiment due to his inability to recruit enough men to fill a company. Not wanting to miss out on action around his home city, he apparently stifled his pride and joined the militia, where again he performed useful services.[16]

By November Washington's tattered army was being hounded across New Jersey by the triumphant British. But even at this low point of the War for Independence the American position was not as dire as textbooks make it appear. On Lake Champlain a large American force entrenched on Mount Independence blocked a British advance. Between there and New York City other American units, with more men than remained with Washington at the time, held the Hudson Highlands, which Washington considered the key to the war. Here was the setting for the next phase of Willett's military adventures, for in November he was given the rank of lieutenant colonel in the Third New York Regiment. The regiment was commanded by Col. Peter Gansevoort, a young man from a respected Dutch family of Albany.

Once again Willett headed up the Hudson into action. He spent the winter of 1776-1777 recruiting, while Washington's main army resisted being driven into oblivion. Working out of Fishkill, Willett and the prospective captains of the Third enjoyed better success than Willett had experienced among his urban neighbors.

In March Willett was ordered to take command of Fort Constitution (later called Fort Independence), located on an island in the Hudson below West Point. The colonel was probably disappointed at being assigned to garrison duty at an uncompleted fort, but the possibility of British attack was always present. On March 23, 1777, a British raiding party of 500 men appeared at Peekskill and drove off a small force of defenders commanded by General McDougall. The general called on Willett, who promptly marched to assist.

Arriving at McDougall's hilltop refuge, Willett noticed a British detachment of about 100 men engaged in burning a house. A steep ravine separated these troops from the main body. With the comprehension that is the mark of a natural military leader, Willett saw that a quick maneuver would cut off this forward detachment. He pleaded with McDougall to let him attack, but the general, formerly one of the boldest Sons of Liberty but perhaps unnerved by his hasty retreat, now showed excess caution. Willett begged to make the attack with his own troops, and McDougall finally conceded. By then the best chance had passed; darkness was approaching, and although Willett moved out with all possible speed, most of the British were able to escape.[17] Nevertheless, Willett's bold move helped convince the raiders to depart and prevented further depredations. His conduct won favorable notice and began building a reputation for courage and audacity.

Willett's men, recruits with only a few months' service, were able to perform effectively because the colonel had used the time to drill and regulate them. Undoubtedly appalled by the chaos he had seen on the invasion of Canada and possibly recalling the rigid organization of the British army, Willett enforced stern discipline. He issued careful, detailed instructions covering all aspects of military life. Determined to build a cohesive, confident fighting force, the former street brawler had become a firm believer in order.

Fort Constitution was probably indefensible. Later in the year it was hurriedly abandoned after stronger nearby positions were taken. Marinus Willett would have won little glory at that picturesque island. Instead, destiny called him to one of the places that would be closely connected with his fame—Fort Stanwix.

As his letters reveal, there was a touch of the poet in Willett's makeup, and it is too bad he did not record his impressions on returning to the Mohawk Valley. It is unlikely he had revisited the area since his agonizing homeward journey as a desperately ill young soldier nearly 20 years earlier. The shape of the valley's future prosperity was already discernible in the 1750s, and two decades of peace had brought greater improvement. Farms and hamlets now lined the river in almost unbroken succession as far as German Flats (now Herkimer) almost 80 miles west of Albany.

As the name German Flats suggests, a conspicuous element in the population consisted of so-called Palatine Germans. These were Protestant inhabitants of the Rhineland who had been displaced and left destitute by the armies of Louis XIV. New York colonial governors had brought 2000 of these refugees from England, initially hoping to employ them to produce naval stores from pitch pine. Left to their own devices in 1712 after this scheme failed, many of the starving Germans settled in the Mohawk and nearby Schoharie Valleys. Like their brethren the "Pennsylvania Dutch," the Palatines earned a reputation as successful farmers; but, although organized into militia, they were considered poor military material. Unlike many other frontier settlers, they had not been obliged to wrest lands from the natives by force.

When Willett had last seen Fort Stanwix in 1758, it was not yet finished; probably it looked better then than it struck the returning colonel on his arrival, May 29, 1777. Earth and log forts of this kind were not intended to be permanent installations. Although the British had brought it to a state of near completion, it had deteriorated rapidly after the peace of 1763. American strategists had immediately perceived the importance of the place and had begun rebuilding it in 1776; but manpower and supplies never seemed to be adequate. The Americans had begun calling it Fort Schuyler, in honor of Gen. Philip Schuyler, but the bulky structure was easier to rename than rebuild.[18]

Willett had scarcely unpacked when he found cause for concern in the work of the French engineer who was supervising the construction. Experience at Fort Constitution had made the colonel suspicious of the abilities of European adventurers who washed up on American shores and whose inflated credentials were received with exaggerated awe. Always quick to jump to conclusions, Willett declared that the engineer was incompetent or perhaps traitorous. He made his case to Colonel Gansevoort, but the commander was not convinced that the Frenchman's work was hopeless.

In an age of excessive sensitivity over pride and rank, there were any number of reasons for Willett and Gansevoort to clash. Willett was nine years older and more experienced in military matters. Gansevoort, like Schuyler, was a member of the Albany aristocracy, although the ancestor in America had come over as a brewer. While

Willett had been brawling in the streets of Manhattan, Gansevoort had been attending Princeton and cultivating a taste for music. Temperamentally, too, they were different: Gansevoort stolid and dutiful, while Willett was active and impulsive.

Peter Gansevoort had been made colonel in the same reorganization of the New York line in November 1776 that gave Willett his rank. Both had served in the Canadian expedition, but it is not certain that they had met before the day Willett strode through the unfinished gate of Fort Stanwix. Against all obstacles, they worked out a relationship; for at heart both were dedicated patriots, and their sense of duty lifted them above personal differences.

Willett had approached insubordination by dashing off a letter to General Schuyler denouncing the engineer; but without the support of Gansevoort, Schuyler would not act. Meanwhile, Willett watched the Frenchman commit blunders such as erecting wooden barracks beyond the walls of the fort, where they would be useless and

Statue of Peter Gansevoort near Fort Stanwix, Rome, New York. The statue was dedicated in 1907, largely through the efforts of Peter Gansevoort's granddaughter, Catherine Gansevoort Lansing.

even dangerous in an attack. He could only stand by and grind his teeth until the engineer had carried his plans to the point where his incompetence would be undeniable. Finally Willett had the satisfaction of seeing the engineer sent downriver in disgrace, but the waste of manpower and materials could not be recovered.

None of this would have mattered if time had been abundant, but time was running out. After the British on Lake Champlain had turned back late in 1776, everyone expected they would renew their offensive from that direction in the following year. One of the British generals in Canada, John Burgoyne, had gone home for the winter and drawn up an elaborate plan for invasion from the north. His fairly detailed descriptions of forces and directions perhaps concealed the flimsy strategic underpinnings of his scheme. Burgoyne's undeniable charm helped gain him the command of the invading army.

As part of his plan, Burgoyne called for a smaller force to move down the Mohawk Valley and join him in victory at Albany. Command of this expedition was given to 40-year-old Lt. Col. Barrimore (Barry) St. Leger, who by the standards of the British officer class had considerable experience in frontier warfare. Although Burgoyne treated this as a diversion, in some ways it made more sense than his primary strategy. The Mohawk region was a rich source of supplies for the Americans and could be equally lucrative for the British. More important, there was reason to expect that many of the inhabitants would support the invaders. Before the war the valley had been dominated by Sir William Johnson, a baronet and superintendent of Indian affairs for the northern colonies. Years of effort cultivating and understanding the Iroquois had kept them in general favorably inclined toward the British. This was especially true of the Mohawks, the easternmost member of the confederation; Johnson was the physical father of a noticeable portion of the Mohawk population. His Mohawk widow, Molly Brant, continued to exert great influence among the Iroquois, whose society gave considerable weight to the counsel of women.

Solemn conferences with the Indians had become increasingly stressful, and it was at one such in 1774 that Johnson suddenly died. This timing was one of those accidents of history that have vast impact. None of Johnson's heirs and successors approached his prestige, and as the troubles with the crown worsened, the patriot faction gained the upper hand. The former "lords of the valley," increasingly suspect, were forced to flee to the safety of Canada, leaving behind most of their possessions.

For the Iroquois this was a terrible time. Many of their leaders, sensing that the war would bring them no good, wanted to remain neutral. But the British, and to a lesser extent the Americans, pressured them to enter the conflict. The Mohawks and Senecas supported the British, while many Oneidas, influenced by a New England missionary, favored the rebels. The strength of the confederacy had been based on consensus, but council after council failed to reach agreement. Finally, the council fire at Onondaga was symbolically covered, leaving each tribe to go its own way.

Promised gifts and loyalty to Sir William Johnson's heirs persuaded hundreds of Indians to join St. Leger at Oswego. Before long, advance Indian scouts were seen lurking around Fort Stanwix, while friendly Oneidas brought news of St. Leger's approach. Members of the garrison who ventured beyond the safety of the fort were likely to be picked off. Capt. James Gregg and a corporal disregarded instructions and good sense and went off to shoot birds. Instead, they were ambushed by Indians, shot and scalped. The corporal died, but Gregg, astonishingly, survived; after a period of convalescence, he served out the remainder of the war.

On another occasion, three girls who lived near the fort were attacked while picking berries. Two were killed and scalped, one of them the daughter of a British soldier who had remained around the ruinous fort while collecting his pension. This incident particularly outraged Gansevoort and Willett, who wrote fiery denunciations of the barbarity. These letters, as intended, may have helped galvanize the Tryon County militia, which until then had seemed dismayingly complacent. By reminding them of what might lay in store if the invaders prevailed, the attack on the berry-pickers may have had much the same effect as the celebrated Jane McCrea incident of the Burgoyne campaign. (Tryon County, formed in 1772 and named for the last royal governor, embraced the vast territory between Albany County and the 1768 treaty line.)

By August 2, 1777, large elements of St. Leger's force, especially Indians, appeared around the fort. Simultaneously, American reinforcements and supplies slipped in at the last possible moment, bringing American troop strength to over 700. (St. Leger's force was at least twice as large, but it is difficult to be sure of precise numbers where so many Indians were present.) St. Leger positioned his troops on August 3; Indians whooped and howled trying to frighten the garrison into quick surrender. The defenders' response was a Continental flag, which had been hastily sewed together and raised from the ramparts that morning. The blue material was taken from a cloak Willett had captured at Peekskill.

Hoping to capitalize on the impression his force had made and filled with contempt for American fighting abilities, the haughty St. Leger delivered a version of the pompous proclamation Burgoyne had issued earlier, promising good treatment if the rebels returned to their royal allegiance. This was brusquely rejected, and with that formality concluded, the British and Indians began firing artillery and small arms and demonstrating around the fort.

Unknown to the garrison, a resolute leader of the Tryon County militia, Gen. Nicholas Herkimer, had mobilized his forces and was marching to relieve the fort. On August 6 three exhausted messengers came into the fort, bringing word that Herkimer was approaching. Gansevoort ordered three cannon to be fired, a prearranged signal to inform Herkimer that his message had been received, and immediately organized a force to create a diversion. Willett was placed in command, but before he could launch his attack a heavy rain shower delayed them.

This same shower had effects elsewhere; for at that moment Herkimer's militia were engaged in a desperate fight for survival. The general had camped near the present village of Oriskany, where he prudently wanted to wait for the confirming shots from the fort. Taunted by officers who accused him of cowardice and disloyalty (an easy accusation to make, since Herkimer had a brother and other relatives with the Tories) the general angrily gave the order to advance. Although he had Oneidas with him, scouting was somehow neglected, and march discipline was atrocious, with long lines of men and wagons strung out along the narrow trail. All the criticisms regulars made of militia were demonstrated, and the result was that Herkimer's army blundered into an ambush about six miles from the fort.

Two factors probably saved the militia from destruction. First, the trap was sprung too soon when Indians began firing prematurely. Many officers, Herkimer included, were shot in the first volley, but many of the troops escaped. Then, with the militia again in danger of being overwhelmed, the rain brought them a respite. They used this godsend to regroup and after that gave a better account of themselves.

None of this was known in the fort, where the only clue that something unusual was happening was the sight of some of the besiegers drawing away. The garrison, however, interpreted this action as a ruse to lure them into an ill-considered attack. Willett mustered his force of 250 men and a small field-piece without knowing what he might encounter.

The National Park Service reconstructed Fort Stanwix in time to open for the 1976 Bicentennial. Willett's attack would have burst out of the sallyport (center), which was then probably extended by a covered passageway.

Any uncertainty Willett felt was not evident to his troops. In characteristic Willett style his raiders burst out of the fort's sally port with seemingly irresistible force. After scattering enemy sentries, they discovered that the camp of Sir John Johnson's Tories and the nearby Indian camp were almost deserted. It became apparent then that most of the enemy had gone off to battle the militia, leaving behind so much loot that Willett sent back to the fort for wagons. Returning after plundering the camps, Willett met a force hastily organized by St. Leger, but these were scattered by effective cannon and musket fire. The raid seemed to be a stunning success, bringing back loads of valuable military supplies, as well as interesting trophies such as flags, letters (including some which the British had intercepted), and the scalps of the two girls who had been killed outside the fort. All this had been accomplished without American casualties, while the enemy suffered several killed.

Willett received great praise, including a sword presented by Congress, for this well-managed exploit. Even the British reports gave him grudging admiration. Apparently he had not been ordered to join the militia battle, about which he knew nothing, and thus could not be criticized for not going further. Gansevoort, cautious, considered that his main responsibility was to hold the fort; therefore he dared not risk bringing his garrison outside the protective walls to join the fray.

Meanwhile, the battle that became known as Oriskany raged with exceptional fury. Inspired by Herkimer's steadiness, the battered militia held on and began to inflict damage. It was one of the most ferocious and personal battles of the war. Fought on the British side largely by Tories and Indians, it pitted angry men against former neighbors, foes they recognized in the heat of combat. For the Iroquois too it was a dark day: the spiritual foundation of the confederacy crumbled as members of different tribes fought each other for the first time in centuries. As part of St. Leger's force pulled back to meet Willett's sally, the militia was left in possession of the bloody field, but they were unable to reach the fort or bring in vital supplies. Herkimer's ruined army dragged back down the valley, never again to appear in such strength.

Later patriotic historians tried to make Oriskany an American victory, even the turning point of the Revolution. No one thought so at the time: the militia crawled away like a mortally wounded animal, and two days later an arrogant British officer entered the fort to offer surrender terms.

It was a moment of intense drama, laden with stage effects: the British delegates remained blindfolded until they entered Gansevoort's quarters. In their darkness the emissaries smelled the odor of fresh-cut boards and heard the nervous rustling of numerous men. The shutters were closed so that the enemy could see nothing of the inside of the fort, and the room was lit only by flickering candlelight. On the table, wine and cheese and crackers were offered in a thin pretense of civility. Gansevoort had filled the room with all the officers who could be spared, so that they could witness the confrontation.

The British major wasted little time in formalities: speaking in a stiff, cold manner, he said that St. Leger was scarcely able to restrain the Indians, who had suffered grievous casualties at Oriskany. If the garrison did not surrender immediately, not only would they be killed, but the warriors threatened "to march down the country, and destroy the settlement, with its inhabitants. In this case, not only men, but women and children will experience the sad effects of their vengeance."

Willett and the other officers endured this in hard-edged silence. When the Englishman had finished, Gansevoort gave Willett permission to reply. Several theories have been advanced as to why Gansevoort did not respond in person. One suggestion is that he was embarrassed by his Dutch accent. Although Dutch was his mother tongue, he had been educated at Princeton, and he seemed to be fluent in English. Another possibility is that protocol prevented the commander from replying to an officer of lower rank. More likely, Gansevoort knew Willett well enough to guess the effect of the major's contemptuous offer and saw that the former streetcorner orator would give the most appropriate response.

Willett's account was first published in his *Narrative*, so his exact words are subject to question.[19] Nevertheless, the language and attitudes are pure Willett and express his blazing hatred of British power, an indignation fanned by the killing of the young girls and now by the major's arrogant demands. More than two years had passed since the civilian Willett had seized the reins in Broad Street. The colonel had experienced a great deal since then and knew that he was engaged in a long and arduous struggle, but the flame burned brighter than ever. As recorded, his reply was a masterpiece of its kind:

> Do I understand you, Sir? I think you say, that you come from a British colonel, who is commander of the army that invests this fort; and by your uniform, you appear to be an officer in the British service. You have made a long speech on the occasion of your visit, which, stript of its superfluities, amounts to this, that you come from a British colonel, to the commandant of this garrison, to tell him, that if he does not deliver up the garrison into the hands of your Colonel, he will send his Indians to murder our women and children. You will please to reflect, sir, that their blood will be on your head, not on ours. We are doing our duty: this garrison is committed to our charge, and we will take care of it. After you get out of it, you may turn around and look at its outside, but never expect to come in again, unless you come a prisoner. I consider the

message you have brought, a degrading one for a British officer to
send, and by no means reputable for a British officer to carry. For
my part, I declare, before I would consent to deliver this garrison
to such a murdering set as your army, by your own account,
consists of, I would suffer my body to be filled with splinters and
set on fire, as you know has at times been practised, by such hordes
of women and children killers, as belong to your army.[20]

A day later Gansevoort made a formal written reply to St. Leger's
demand: "It is my determined resolution. . . to defend this fort and
garrison to the last extremity, in behalf of the United American
States, who have placed me here to defend it against all their enemies."
This proud and defiant retort may be more impressive to us than it
was at the time. Such statements were an accepted element of the
ritual of sieges. Within memory of many of those present at Fort
Stanwix, the British had delivered a similar reply at Fort William
Henry, only to surrender a few days later.

By the time this brusque dismissal was delivered into St. Leger's
refined hand, Marinus Willett was no longer at Fort Stanwix. He had
gone off on the most dangerous and weighty of all his exploits.
Although Gansevoort and Willett had brazenly defied St. Leger, they
understood that the fort, crowded with more men than it could
comfortably accommodate and incompletely restored, could not
hold out for a long siege. Outside aid would be needed, and it was
clear that the Tryon County militia would not be able to provide it.
Willett then volunteered to go down and secure help, taking with
him a lieutenant, Levi Stockwell, who was known as a skilled
woodsman.

The enemy surrounded the fort, meaning that the two officers
would have to slip through their lines. If captured, they could have
no illusions about the outcome. Willett's mention of being burned
alive by splinters showed that he was familiar with a common Indian
method of torture. He had seen Captain Gregg "weltering in his
gore." Rank would offer little protection to a man who had shaken
his fist in the face of a British officer and called him a murderer.

Even in a time when an infant nation's military structure was
much looser than today, it was extraordinary for a colonel, second
in command, to go forth on a critical individual mission. Analysts
might suspect that there was dissension between Gansevoort and

Willett, but the record does not support this surmise. More likely the explanation offered by Willett is correct: in his brief passage through the valley, the Tryon militia had "expressed a particular attachment" to him.[21] The importance of this errand can hardly be overestimated. A little over a month before, Fort Ticonderoga had fallen to Burgoyne with dismaying ease. Only in retrospect would it become apparent that the value and impregnability of the "Gibraltar of the North" was overrated. At the time it seemed that little stood in the path of the invincible Burgoyne; perhaps he was already in Albany, as St. Leger's emissary had suggested. Willett and Stockwell went forth in a dark hour of the night and a dark time for the Northern Department.

Armed only with long spears known as spontoons, the two men slipped out of the sally port in the midnight stillness. In the thick damp air they sensed the nearness of the river, which they crossed by crawling along a log. Surrounded by the swampy darkness, they soon lost their sense of direction. They knew, however, that the Indians were camped nearby, and when they heard a dog bark, Stockwell felt

The Mohawk River from the Willett Bridge, near where Willett and Stockwell made their hazardous crossing. The photo was taken at approximately the same time of year, but the flow of water in the Mohawk may be much reduced from the eighteenth century by the construction of Delta Dam upstream.

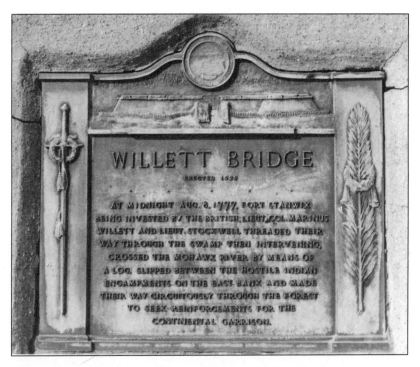

Plaque on the Willett Memorial Bridge, which carries East Dominick Street over the Mohawk River at Rome, New York.

they had no choice but to stand perfectly still against a tree until the light increased. It seemed like an eternity of waiting, and indeed lasted several hours until daylight approached.

Luck favored them, and they passed undetected through the enemy lines. They had carried no blankets and no food other than pocketsful of cheese and crackers and a canteen of spirits. Still in the wilderness, another night overtook them. Soaked from stepping in and out of the river to hide their trail and hungry, the two officers spent a chill night wrapped in each other's arms to keep warm. Willett awoke with severe rheumatism and limped the rest of the 50-mile journey to Fort Dayton. Even the British were forced to praise this daring exploit.

At Fort Dayton Willett learned that General Schuyler had already sent relief to the fort named in his honor. Schuyler had taken a great risk in dispatching part of his depleted force up the Mohawk,

and this courageous decision further antagonized the New England-
ers. Willett and Stockwell rode down the valley to meet the first
section of the relief force, then continued to Albany where they met
the tempestuous Gen. Benedict Arnold, who had been placed in
overall command of the expedition.

Willett returned to Fort Dayton with Arnold and there attended
to two other matters. First, he visited General Herkimer, whose
wounded leg had been amputated. The gallant general appeared to be
in good spirits when Willett visited, but bled to death later that night,
due, it was widely believed, to incompetent medical treatment.
During Willett's absence, Walter Butler, a young man whose intense
Tory attitudes had caused him to flee the Mohawk Valley and had
returned with St. Leger, had ventured out on an amazingly nervy
errand. He had been captured in a tavern while conducting a public
meeting of Tory sympathizers. Arnold asked Willett to serve as judge
advocate at the trial on August 20. Butler was found guilty and
sentenced to death; but he had been popular before the war, and some
American officers pleaded for clemency, which Arnold granted.
Instead of being hanged, Butler was placed in loose confinement in
Albany.

Willett was fully aware of the effect his secret departure might
have on the tenuous morale of the besieged garrison. With this in
mind, he wrote an address to his "companions in arms" to be read
the next day. In this characteristically passionate document, Willett
pleaded "Let no man's heart fail him, tho he is surrounded with a sett
of Cruel Savage Enemies; there Cruelty & Vengence should cause us
to double our Fortitude & Diligence." In an inspiring conclusion he
told his comrades:

> I beseech you by all the love and regard you have for yourselves
> for your Countrey, and all the regard you have for me to persevere
> in doing your Duty like good Soldiers. Dont be afraid of your
> Enemies. They are truly a Contemptable pack,—their designs are
> of the most barbarious kind, but their power is not sufficient to
> put there Diabolical purposes into execution—do your duty and
> fear not, but God Almighty will bless you with success eaqual to
> your most Sanguin hopes.[22]

Perhaps this defiant message helped sustain the isolated garrison.
After failing to frighten the Americans into surrender, St. Leger

commenced formal siege operations. The siege that had been expected at Ticonderoga took place on a smaller scale at Fort Stanwix. Having expected little resistance, St. Leger had brought only light artillery. He soon learned, as he later wrote, that "our cannon had not the least effect upon the sodwork of the fort, and that our royals [mortars] had only the power of teasing . . . ." St. Leger then resorted to digging zigzag trenches to bring his guns and marksmen closer to the fort and was making slow progress. If St. Leger could have maintained a long siege, Gansevoort's position might have become ominous; his men were crowded into a fort with poor sanitation and ever-decreasing supplies of food and ammunition. Eventually, he might have been faced with a choice of surrender or trying to break out.

Not wanting to repeat Herkimer's misfortune, the audacious Arnold showed unusual caution until he or someone else conceived a clever ruse. A young Tory named Hon Yost Schuyler—mentally defective according to some accounts—had been captured with Walter Butler. Facing death, he was given a chance for reprieve by carrying a message to the Indians in St. Leger's army that Arnold was approaching with overwhelming force. Historians differ on the impact of Hon Yost's ploy. The Iroquois by then were thoroughly tired of the siege: it was not their method of warfare; they had suffered casualties, and instead of making off with easy plunder, their own possessions had been looted by Willett.

Hon Yost Schuyler's ruse had the desired effect—or gave the Indians the excuse they needed. When Arnold arrived on August 22, 1777, he found that the besieging army had fled in disorder. For Burgoyne this was a severe setback. Almost simultaneously, he suffered a defeat at Bennington. Slowed by Philip Schuyler's delaying tactics, deserted by most of his Indian auxiliaries and confronted by an increasingly powerful foe, the once-pompous general saw himself beset by adversity.

The homemade flag still flew above Fort Stanwix and the garrison, in the words of one young officer, was "once more at Liberty to walk about and take the free Air we had for 21 days been Deprived of."[23] Gansevoort went eagerly down the valley to visit his beloved fiancee, Caty Van Schaick, leaving Willett in command. There was reason to fear that the British would return, and Willett used this interval to rebuild discipline, as well as the fort structure, and write urgent letters to demand more supplies.

In late September, after Gansevoort returned, Willett himself headed south to visit his family. He reached Albany after the first battle of Saratoga, in which the Americans, now commanded by Horatio Gates, stopped Burgoyne's attack. Burgoyne begged for help from Sir Henry Clinton in New York City, and Clinton finally responded with a move up the Hudson just as Willett was traveling downstream to visit his wife. On October 6, Willett wrote to Gansevoort from Fishkill: "It is now Eleven days since I left you & have not yet had the pleasure of seeing Mrs. Willett. . . . The enemy are now at Peeks Kill & this Countrey in Alarm."[24] Shortly afterward, Clinton captured the Highlands forts, with heavy American losses.

This, however, marked nearly the high tide of the British advance up the Hudson. Clinton, ever cautious, dared not do more than create a diversion in Burgoyne's behalf. After another unsuccessful assault on the American position, Burgoyne capitulated on October 17, a great turning point of the war. Willett, Gansevoort and all those who had stood fast at Fort Stanwix could take pride in their achievement, an astonishing reversal of fortune in the 15 weeks since the beaten Americans had slunk out of Ticonderoga.

III. CONTINENTAL

And in serving my country I have served a cause in which my whole soul is most fairly engaged. —Marinus Willett, April 1, 1781.[25]

WILLETT was still around Fishkill when Burgoyne laid down his arms. With the Third New York facing a winter of inactivity at a frontier fort, Gansevoort gave his deputy leave to travel to Philadelphia. The capital had already fallen to the British, and Willett joined the American army at its camp at White Marsh early in November. This may have been his first meeting with Washington, whom he had long admired. The New Yorker observed what he could of the "Grand armey" and cheered the brave defenders of Fort Mifflin on the Delaware. This poorly built structure had to be abandoned on November 15. Washington's army began its terrible encampment at Valley Forge, and by January Willett was back at Fort Stanwix.

Between Valley Forge and the Mohawk Valley, Willett visited Mary at Danbury, Connecticut, an important American base, where she had been forced to take refuge after the British occupied New York. He improved the occasion by dashing off an urgent letter to George Clinton, New York's first governor under its independent constitution. Clinton was also a general, but his reputation had been tarnished by losing the Highlands forts. Like Willett, he had been a prewar radical, and they knew each other well enough to communicate frankly.

In a letter altogether typical of Willett's restless energy and urge to action, he proposed a surprise attack on British-held New York City while the main enemy army was occupying Philadelphia. Admitting that "the scheme of attempting to take a place where there are 7000 men with 8000 has the appearance of rashness, and may in some cases deserve the appelation of stupidity," he argued that the British troops were dispersed and many were new recruits, inadequately trained and motivated. Willett had considered the tactical problems and advised that "Three things are necessary for the execution of enterprises of this nature[:] *Materials, Secrecy* and *Vigor*."[26]

During the remainder of the war Governor Clinton demonstrated perseverance and resourcefulness that were almost superhuman, but Willett's proposal caught him in a moment of dejection. He replied that secrecy was essential, but that it was "morally impossible" to achieve where militia were concerned.[27] Willett's bold initiative thus was never tried. The colonel, obviously, was eager to recover his property in New York and end Mary's refugee wandering, but Clinton would have been equally pleased to regain the metropolis of his shrunken realm. Even if the city had been captured, it is unlikely it could have been defended against a British counterattack supported by the navy with any better success than in '76.

Back at Fort Stanwix after his interlude with the main army, Willett was in a "How're you gonna keep 'em down on the farm" position. He was not alone in chafing under routine inactivity at a frontier outpost. On February 26, 1778, virtually all the officers of the Third New York, weary of "perpetual fatigue, which may be conceived rather a disgrace than honor to a Soldier," petitioned Gansevoort to be transferred to the Grand Army during the ensuing campaign, so as to "learn that Art of War, so essential for the Accomplishment of every good Officer."[28] Knowing Willett's talent for rabble-rousing, it is tempting to surmise that he was a leader of this movement, but he had been back at Fort Stanwix only a few days when the petition was drafted.

Gansevoort rebuffed the plea, but he was not altogether unsympathetic to the yearning of his officers. Meanwhile, the commandant went off to marry Caty, leaving Willett in charge of the discontented garrison. There were few instances in which Continental regiments were stationed permanently at a frontier fort, which confirmed the exceptional importance the American leadership attached to maintaining a strong presence at the gateway to the rich Mohawk Valley.

A major incentive was to provide visible support for the two Iroquois tribes that generally favored the Americans and to have a base from which to influence the other members of the fragmented confederacy. Fort Stanwix lay beyond the frontier of settlement, on what was a national frontier that the United States still respected. The fort was the beginning point for the line agreed at the treaty of 1768; beyond extended the mysterious realm of Iroquoia.

A large part of Willett's duties consisted of diplomacy with the nearby Iroquois. For a city-bred man, he had a flair for this task. He understood the convoluted, formal wording and elaborate flattery that were traditional in negotiations with the natives. When he addressed their representatives as "Brother Warriors" and invoked the warrior code, his reputation made his words credible. On May 12, 1778, Colonel Willett had the pleasant duty of informing the Indians of the alliance that had been concluded with France. "This great addition of our strength must make us more than a match for our inveterate enemies. . . . I make no doubt but you will rejoice with us on this happy occasion," he declared.[29]

On his return Gansevoort, sensitive to his subordinate's urge to operate in a larger sphere, released Willett to visit Washington's army. According to Willett's narrative, Gansevoort had entrusted him to ask Washington to transfer the regiment to a more active theater. Arriving at Peekskill on June 21, Willett met General Gates, and the northern commander sent him as a messenger to carry a dispatch to Washington. This also gave Willett another opportunity to visit Marinus, Jr., an active and promising youth of 16 who was serving as surgeon's mate with the main army.

After a futile winter in Philadelphia, the British army was withdrawing across New Jersey. A hard day's ride brought Willett to Washington's field camp. After delivering his message, he obtained the commander's permission to remain with the army. Willett was not given command of troops, but was attached as an aide to General Charles Scott, a craggy Virginian with whom Willett probably hit it off instantly.

Largely by accident, Willett was granted his wish to observe the Grand Army, having been tempered at Valley Forge by deprivation and by the training administered by Friedrich Von Steuben. He was present at Monmouth, where on June 28, 1778, Washington's attempt to interrupt the British retreat to the safety of New York brought on the last major battle of the war in the North. Under conditions of extreme heat and dust, Willett saw the erratic Gen. Charles Lee disgrace himself and nearly lose the Continental Army until Washington rode up to save the situation. On the battlefield, Willett even had occasion to caution the commander that he was offering too obvious a target. In retrospect Willett said of Washington, "I have seen him in a variety of situations, and none in which he did not appear great; but never did I see him when he exhibited such greatness as on this day."[30]

While Monmouth was being fought to a conclusion indecisive except as an American morale-booster, a much different kind of war was raging on the Northern Frontier. Most American strategists probably assumed that the lesson the British would learn from St. Leger's fiasco of 1777 would be to return with a larger force and heavier guns. In fact, St. Leger's invasion proved to be the last time a large body of regular soldiers came into the valley to conduct a conventional campaign. Instead, an increasingly savage warfare was carried on by Tories and Indians, supported by British army posts. These attacks were led by men such as Sir John Johnson—Sir William's son—John Butler and, most dreaded of all, Joseph Brant (Thayandanegea). A brother of William Johnson's favorite, Molly, Brant had been given a European-style education and other preferential treatment. A dedicated loyalist, he combined British strategic sense with Indian tactics, a deadly combination. If this coven was not already sufficiently ominous, Walter Butler escaped in mid-April 1778 from his loose confinement in Albany, almost certainly aided by collusion. Hardened by imprisonment and embittered by the mistreatment he believed his family had received, he reached Canada seething with dreams of revenge.

While the main armies were marching across New Jersey, John Butler was leading a large raid against American settlements in the Wyoming Valley of northeast Pennsylvania, an area inhabited largely by Connecticut people. He won a crushing victory over the valley's defenders, followed by what Americans considered to be a massacre. Meanwhile, Brant was active in lower New York State, and in July conducted a large raid near German Flats.

Brant maintained a base at a semi-permanent Indian town of Oquaga on the Susquehanna. Palatine militia Colonel Jacob Klock and others recommended that bases such as this be destroyed, as they had become a "receptacle" for runaways and troublemakers.[31] Governor Clinton, anxious to relieve the distress of the frontier, agreed and proposed Colonel Willett to lead the expedition. General Gates, meanwhile, had in mind putting Willett in charge of a larger expedition to chastise the western Iroquois.[32] For reasons that are unclear, Willett was never formally offered either of these commands. In October 1778 Col. William Butler destroyed Oquaga and the other Unadilla settlements, a successful operation that brought more severe retaliation. Many British and American officers conspired actively to secure choice commands. Willett may not even have been aware that he was being proposed. His recommendation was based on his reputation for enterprise and courage.

On his return journey he paused again to visit Mary at Danbury and there they received a letter from Dr. Charles McKnight that would test his fortitude to the utmost:

> Princeton, July 14th, 1778
> It is with the deepest Regret and Contrition of Heart, that I conform to the necessity of transmitting you the most melancholy piece of Intelligence that ever touched the soul of so loving, indulgent and affectionate a Parent. A Day or two after your departure from Corryell's Ferry [PA], Marinus was taken very unwell. He took some medicine which relieved him so much that he went to the River, fishing, where he improperly, when warm, with the other Gentlemen, stripped to swim. Immediately coming out of the Water, he was taken very ill, tho' the Symptoms not being immediately alarming, he would not consent that I should be sent for, as the Gentlemen with him took the Greatest Care of him, 'till Saturday the 11th Instant, at seven in the Eve., he desired to see me, and an Express came off to me at Princeton. I set out immediately with him, but a Parent's Feelings could only equal the distress of my Soul at finding my Dear Marinus, a corpse! I lament your situation, and that of his disconsolate Mother, my own is nothing inferior, in the Loss of him who had by his amiable Disposition, his agreeable Deportment and Manners endeared himself to me by the Strongest bonds of affection . . . . [33]

Young Marinus was a casualty of the war as surely as the farmers who blundered into the fatal ravine at Oriskany. Only on rare occasions did his father reveal some hint of his anguish. Still at Danbury on August 29, he confessed in a letter to Gansevoort, "I am glad my presence is not required at Fort Schuyler as the awfull breach that has taken place in my little famaly has as disjointed it as to render what remains unfit for the necessary duties. The unhappy situation of my dear wife especially requires as much of my company and assistance as possible."[34] There is something poignant in Willett's congratulation to Peter Gansevoort on the birth of his first son: "May he live to be a very lasting Blessing to his Parents."[35] On another occasion a friend who had seen Mary Willett wrote, "When she mentioned her child, she made my heart ache, excuse my freedom."[36] Her pain must have been even more agonizing because only a few weeks earlier, having been told by young Marinus that disease was raging in the hospital, pleaded "I would not have you go in the General Hospital if it is so very sickly."[37]

Washington had made vague promises to Willett to try to transfer the Third New York; for the present it remained at Fort Stanwix. It must have been especially dispiriting for Willett to return to the grim bastion. Though it was high summer, conditions at the fort were particularly gloomy. With increasing boldness, Indians prowled the perimeter, ready to scalp unwary members of the garrison. Officers—like Willett—could be granted leave, or in desperate cases, even resign. For the enlisted men, the only alternative was desertion. A large group had done just that, and on August 15, five recaptured deserters were shot after a court-martial. All the officers present, who had recently presented another petition for transfer, recommended carrying out the sentence. Willett, still at Danbury, was not present during this episode. Probably his belief in firm discipline would have led him to concur.[38]

Colonel Gansevoort had sought the command of the fort that protected the important settlement of Cherry Valley. Instead, it was given to a less competent officer who was surprised and killed in a violent attack by Brant and Walter Butler. Widely publicized as a massacre, the raid shocked the frontier by its lateness in the season (November 11) and its ferocity. Soon the already overburdened Governor Clinton was deluged with appeals for help from the terrorized region.

Clinton feared, as he told Washington, that Tryon County would be depopulated if the inhabitants could not be protected, depriving the state of a major source of grain. This was precisely the result the British were seeking. Desperate to hold the frontier together, Clinton thought of his redoubtable friend, Marinus Willett. Noting that Willett "has an Influence among the People of Tryon County from his Exertions at Fort Schuyler when invested by St. Leger," he requested Washington to release him for service in "arranging the militia."[39] With the commander-in-chief's permission, Clinton on March 15, 1779, tendered the command of a new militia regiment to Colonel Willett.[40]

Now that he was an officer and a gentleman, Willett had adopted the exaggerated personal sensitivity characteristic of that class. Due to the inconsistent manner in which state and Continental commissions had been handed out, complicated by the claims of foreign adventurers, the American officer class was kept in constant turmoil over issues of rank and seniority. Few of them were able to put devotion to the cause ahead of personal vanity, and the outpouring of complaints and accusations based on wounded pride can be disillusioning to the modern reader.

Willett was not immune to the epidemic of hypersensitivity and was already nurturing a grievance because of the elevation of a little-known French-Canadian officer, Pierre Regnier deRoussy, over himself and his friend Col. Frederick Weissenfels. "The bear Idea of being Lt. Col. Com'dt of a Regiment of Militia, while Lt. Col. Regnier, who stands much lower in the N.York Line than I do, is Commandant of a Continental Regt. in the same State is attended with very disagreeable Sensations," he replied to Clinton's offer. Fuming, he added that "if the Promotion of Col. Regnier is confirmed, it is my Intention to retire to some business where I may have an opportunity of freeing myself from such disagreeable embarrasements as I unfortunatly Labour under at present."[41] Willett neither accepted the temporary command nor resigned; perhaps his protest had made the point.

At last the highest levels of government heeded the cries of the frontier and determined to take action in 1779. General Washington shared the frontier belief that the best method of dealing with the Indian menace was to destroy their ability to wage war by ravaging their settlements and crops. Accepting the risk that the British army in New York City would remain dormant, Washington prepared to invade the Iroquois heartland. General John Sullivan of New Hampshire was placed in command of the largest offensive the United States had yet undertaken. Sullivan's earlier and subsequent military career was undistinguished, but, dreading ambush, he conducted this campaign with elaborate care.

Before attacking the western Iroquois, especially the Senecas who were the strongest and most firmly pro-British, the Americans decided to neutralize the Onondagas. Col. Gosen Van Schaick of the First New York, a cousin of Peter Gansevoort's Caty and in command of Fort Stanwix after the Third New York had at long last been relieved in November 1778, led the raid. Willett, though not part of Van Schaick's unit, was called up from Albany specifically to be second-in-command of the strike force. Moving with considerable alacrity, the attackers overcame obstacles of weather and terrain and achieved a degree of surprise when they reached the Onondaga settlements around present Syracuse on April 21, 1779.

The expedition killed about 12 Indians, captured 33 others, and destroyed the villages with their equipment and food supplies without losing a man. From a military standpoint it was a neat operation; but, as with the larger expedition it foreshadowed, the consequences were dubious. The Onondagas in general seem to have preferred neutrality and might have been happy to stay out of the conflict. Van Schaick's attack pushed them into vengeful hostility.

Plans called for Sullivan to be joined by regiments from the Mohawk Valley commanded by General James Clinton, the governor's brother. One of these regiments was the Third New York, which made Gansevoort and Willett part of the expedition. Clinton's division, loaded with supplies for the entire army, had to make a laborious portage to Otsego Lake. From there Clinton employed a familiar lumbermen's tactic. He dammed the outlet of the lake to build a head of water, then floated his division down the Susquehanna, meeting Sullivan at Tioga on August 22. This phase of the campaign had a holiday aspect, but immense work had been necessary. General Clinton wrote that due to the "extraordinary exertions of Lt. Col. Willett," he had been able to transport 120 boats and more than 1200 barrels of provisions.[42] Willett's reputation emphasized his daring exploits, but it was his persistent energy and attention to organizational details that made him an exceptional officer.

Dependent on an impoverished nation for supplies and delayed by the need to hack a road through the wilderness of the Poconos, Sullivan fell weeks behind schedule. He did not leave Tioga until August 26, but thereafter his army moved with ponderous regularity. Only once did the Tories and Indians stand to fight; and then they were brushed aside, though American mismanagement lost a chance for an overwhelming victory.[43] Sullivan reached the Genesee country, relentlessly destroying Seneca crops and villages.

Before departing, Peter Gansevoort wrote Caty, "when we shall have the pleasure of hearing from each other again God only knows, as we shall for some time travel through the wild wilderness where it is not probable an express will find us. . . . "[44] For this reason no Gansevoort or Willett letters from the campaign are extant, and Willett's *Narrative* dismisses it in one sentence. Based on his later writings and actions, it is quite likely he did not regard this as the best method of dealing with the Indians. Given his enormous admiration for Washington, it must have been disturbing that the policy of devastation had come directly from the commander-in-chief.

Fort Niagara was the source of supply for the Indian and Tory raids, but it was far too late in the season for Sullivan to contemplate an attack on it; nor did he have the necessary artillery. Before setting off on the campaign, Gansevoort had expressed his hopes to Caty that the hardships he was about to endure would be justified: "We shall have it in our power to oblige the cruel and inhuman savages to make peace with us on our own terms and thereby securing peace to our destroyed inhabitants on our Frontiers."[45] The actual results were quite different: true, the Iroquois lost their means of livelihood, and perhaps the depredations weakened them in the long term; but for the present the invasion made them both more dependent on British aid and more angry. Perhaps the most lasting consequence of the expedition was to serve as something of a real estate familiarization tour; after the war American soldiers who had seen the previously hidden region for the first time swarmed in to settle.

The campaign had enabled Willett to make unfortunate comparisons between his unit and those from other states. One of his first acts on being restored to a source of writing materials and regular expresses at Easton, Pennsylvania, was to dash off a letter to Governor Clinton complaining of the state's failure to provide adequately for its officers. In his usual hasty, impulsive and frank style, he protested that "We have officers now with our Regiment who cant do Duty meerly for want of Clothes fit to appear upon the parade. What a pitiable situation is this?"[46]

Both Willett and Gansevoort had been taken ill with digestive ailments during the campaign. Willett recovered enough to remain on duty, but Gansevoort returned to Albany for a long convalescence. After marching to the vicinity of the Hudson Highlands, the army settled into winter quarters around Morristown, New Jersey. The coldest winter within memory arrived early, and the soldiers endured great hardships in building log huts. Willett's organizational ability served him well, and his reports to Gansevoort presented a cheerful outlook under the circumstances.

Gansevoort remained at home in Albany despite orders from Congress and General Washington for officers to return to their regiments. At one point the hero of Fort Stanwix was reduced to sending what amounted to a doctor's excuse to explain his absence.[47] Willett remained in charge of the regiment and defended his colonel against the suspicion of malingering and against seemingly unfair charges resulting from an inspection by his nemesis deRoussy.[48] Gansevoort, while regretting his absence, had good reason to observe that "it alleviates my distress when I consider that the command of the Regiment will be left with a person in whom I can confide."[49] Willett in turn, using the Dutch form of the name, extended "a shake of the hand to young Harmanus," the Gansevoorts's newborn son.[50]

The extreme cold froze New York harbor and created the opportunity for the British and Americans to raid each other's positions. Washington saw possibilities of seizing much-needed supplies from British-controlled territory. Not surprisingly Willett, who had become identified as the master of the intrepid foray, came to the forefront. He led a quick raid on Staten Island, during which he reported capturing 17 wagonloads of valuable stores.[51] This apparently was a separate operation from the larger and rather unsuccessful expedition to Staten Island led by "Lord" Stirling on January 14-15, 1780. Willett also reported leading a smaller attack against Paulus Hook, now in Jersey City. Proposals for retaliatory raids by Willett and Col. Moses Hazen, another energetic officer, continued as long as the ice lasted.[52] Willett mentioned receiving an injury to his leg on March 20, but it is not certain whether it occurred in action.[53]

As the terrible weather finally eased, Willett turned his thoughts to the coming campaign. Informing the Quartermaster General that his leg was recovering so that "I hope in a few days to be able to go abroad," he requested to have his saddle finished. He also asked to have a leather horse canteen repaired and "As the season for taking the field is fast approaching," he requested a new camp cot. The one he had "has afforded me a lodging [for] four campaigns, but is now wholly unfit for use." Willett's equipment had seen hard service, to be sure! Under the circumstances, his requests were minimal; his strict integrity did not allow him to profit from his rank as did many others.

Early in 1780 Willett was granted a long-held desire, though under conditions that diminished the satisfaction. He was placed in command of the Fifth New York Regiment, but this was a damaged unit because so many of its officers and men had been captured during Sir Henry Clinton's assault on the Highlands forts in October 1777. An inspection conducted as late as September 6, 1780, found that the regiment "still labours under Considerable Inconvenience from having many of its officers Prisoners of War." The same report found that the unit's clothing was "Equally bad with the other Regts." At that time the regiment had only 194 rank and file present and accounted for and was considered to need 310 men to complete its strength.[54] Command of this diminished regiment earned Willett the rank of full colonel, made effective December 22, 1779, the date the previous commanding officer resigned.[55]

Talk of disbanding or consolidating the weakened regiment inspired Willett to pen another passionate letter, directed to the state's delegates in the Continental Congress. These impulsive outpourings reveal a great deal about Willett's character, especially his recognition of the human factors in war. Noting that "The soldiers of this regiment appear to have a very great attachment to the few officers they have with them," he cautioned that "to separate them will ever be attended with disagreeable consequences." From the officer's point of view, reduction of the regiment would "punish several good officers with a set of tormenting sensations in being sent home just as the army is called upon to face there enemies. God forbid this should be the case. . . . It would be as bad as willfull murder to do it now."[56]

Willett's impassioned plea, accompanied by a memorial from the other officers, accomplished its purpose for the moment. The regiment remained on duty, but saw little action. In 1780 the most intense fighting shifted to the southern theater. Washington lacked the strength to attack the British in New York City, while Sir Henry Clinton, passive by nature, was not inclined to take the offensive.

Willett and his officers tried to fill the vacant ranks of the Fifth New York, but recruiting by that stage of the war was a thankless business. By then the Continental currency had virtually collapsed, and even with French aid the government and its military operations could barely be kept afloat. To the officers, difficulty in recruiting was perhaps not their most pressing concern. As the currency depreciated toward utter worthlessness, unrest spread among both officer and enlisted ranks. Finally, in September 1780 a large majority of the officers in the state's Continental regiments brought their grievances to the legislature. Three officers were chosen to present the petition, one of whom was Willett. Clearly these colleagues saw something they liked in the rugged, plain-spoken Son of Liberty who had, in what already seemed a remote age, harangued the Manhattan crowds and blazed defiance at a supercilious British officer.

The petition called attention to the "unhappy & distressing situation of the Troops under our Command," many of whom had not been paid since January. While the officers had been paid, it was with money whose value was plunging toward oblivion. Their confidence in the currency was gone, and they asked for compensation in lands. "When we say landed Interest, we mean, Gentlemen, improved Estates, such as have a real and immediate value." They meant by this, estates to be confiscated from Tories who had fled the state.[57] This petition, with its implied threat, presumably hastened the confiscation process, from which many officers eventually benefited.

Being prominently associated with this protest may not have helped Willett's career. Officers' gossip must have brought word that Congress was again discussing a consolidation of the Continental regiments. However much troops were needed, a destitute government could no longer maintain them. Foreseeing this possibility, Willett apparently wrote to Washington offering to form or join some sort of independent regiment. Washington replied that while "It will give me great pleasure to see an Officer of your merit retained in service. . . I have not heard any thing of the formation of a Legion."[58] The dreaded blow fell on January 1, 1781, when the number of New York regiments was reduced from five to two. Willett, lacking the seniority of other officers, was out of a job.

For five campaigns Marinus Willett's life had been one of action and frequent danger. Suddenly he was idle. The cause he served with his whole soul and for which his son had died was neither won nor lost, but he was excluded from participation. Back in Danbury, he encountered daily Mary's profound sorrow over the loss of their son and their home, the depression caused by years of a refugee's insecurity. Financial distress added to his gloom; deprived of military benefits (even if the pay was of little value) he saw no practical means of earning a living as long as the British occupied New York City and threatened the rest of the state. As the customary spring campaigning season arrived and he remained inactive, he brooded over the ill-treatment he had received.

At this low point his old resentment of the powerful returned, and he began to suspect that some of those who were on the same side were conspiring against him. At last the torment became insupportable and, on April 1, 1781, Willett responded with one of his characteristic letters, a 17-page rush of unfiltered emotion directed to the New York delegates in Congress. Provoked by the belief that he had been dismissed to make place for others, he wrote, "It is difficult, gentlemen, to conceive what must be my feelings when I look around and see that the cards have been stacked upon me, and that I have been compleately cheated." His anger centered on the supposition that "my old competitor" Col. Lewis Dubois had been given leave to form a new regiment—just after Willett's had been disbanded. (Dubois had resigned the command of the Fifth New York in December 1779, creating the vacancy later filled by Willett.) Willett also freely admitted his financial distress, made more acute by failure to pay him for past services. "I stand in direct and immediate need of what is due to me, and little as it is I shall be very glad to receive it."[59]

Yet within a month Willett's career had taken a new direction, and instead of being cast aside he was on his way to the scene of his greatest service. Governor Clinton more than two years earlier had thought of placing Willett in charge of defending the Mohawk Valley. Now, with the fear of leaving a disgruntled Colonel Willett smoldering in his rear as an additional factor, the Governor pleaded with him to accept the command. For the colonel it was a major blow to pride to exchange rank in a Continental regiment for command of raw levies and militia. (If it was any consolation, Peter Gansevoort was in the same position and also accepted a militia command.) Under ordinary circumstances Willett might have refused even the urgent pleas of his friend, but these were exceptional times, with Willett's ability to support himself and his wife no small consideration. Thus in April 1781 the man who would become the savior of the Mohawk Valley once again fastened his epaulets and buckled his sword.

IV. THE SAVIOR OF THE MOHAWK VALLEY

The present distressed situation of the inhabitants, is such as to demand sympathy from the most unfeeling heart. —Willett to Washington, July 6, 1781.

ACCORDING TO STANDARD HISTORIES, the war in the North largely subsided after the battle of Monmouth. Washington's army and the British in New York stalked each other without being able to inflict severe damage. To the Mohawk Valley, this notion of placid equilibrium was a cruel deception. Any expectation that the Sullivan campaign would bring security to the frontier was quickly shattered. Huddled in makeshift shelters around Fort Niagara, the displaced Iroquois suffered through the same severe weather as the troops at Morristown. Their rage fanned by British and Tory officers using them for their own strategic purposes, the warriors burst forth on their mission of devastation earlier than usual. In April 1780 Brant was raiding south of the Mohawk, penetrating as far as Minisink on the Delaware, almost to the tip of New Jersey. In retaliation for helping the Americans, the Oneida villages were systematically destroyed. This completed the devastation of Iroquoia and left the Mohawk Valley settlements without their screen of scouts.

Facing page: **New England artist Ralph Earl painted this conventional portrait of Willett around 1791. The Colonel is wearing the sword awarded him by Congress and a badge of the Society of the Cincinnati. In keeping with the stylized portraiture of the day, Earl added a couple of symbolic Indians in the background. The painting may be an accurate depiction of Willett's appearance but fails somehow to capture his character.** Courtesy of The Metropolitan Museum of Art, Bequest of George Willett Van Nest, 1917 [17.87.1]

Sir John Johnson led a major attack in the Johnstown area in May. After Brant wrought great damage around Canajoharie in August, Johnson led another invasion in October. Simultaneously, Maj. Guy Carleton attacked down Lake Champlain; possibly these movements were intended to coincide with Benedict Arnold's planned betrayal of West Point in a renewal of the strategy of 1777. In response, militia Gen. Robert Van Rensselaer gathered a large force, the most impressive home army assembled since Oriskany. In a battle on October 19, the Americans gained the advantage, but when it seemed that Van Rensselaer was in position to crush the invaders, he withdrew and allowed them to escape. His sluggishness was also responsible for the death of Col. John Brown of Massachusetts, a brave fighter on the order of Willett, and for the sacrifice of a party sent from Fort Stanwix to Oneida Lake to destroy Johnson's boats. Van Rensselaer's noble name protected him from richly deserved censure by a court of inquiry, but the outcome was immensely disheartening to the populace. As the grim year 1780 closed, the biggest problem for the raiders was finding targets that had not already been ravaged.

Above: **A New York State historical marker located about two miles north of Palatine Bridge points out the battle in which Col. John Brown of Massachusetts was killed. Brown was an intrepid fighter who had performed brilliantly during the Burgoyne campaign, and his loss was deeply felt.**

Five years of incessant conflict had nearly ruined the rich valley and shattered the morale of its remaining inhabitants. The frightful losses at Oriskany had not been—could not be—replaced. At the close of 1780, according to one account, Tryon County reported 700 buildings had been burned, 354 families had abandoned their homes, 613 persons had deserted to the enemy, 197 had been killed, 121 taken captive, 1200 farms were uncultivated because of enemy action, 300 women had been widowed and 1200 children orphaned.[60] No other region of the United States had suffered such sustained and terrible losses. A land nature had intended to be lovely and bountiful had been turned into a bloodstained, fearful place. Instead of solid home-steads surrounded by rich fields, a succession of 24 ominous forts marked the route up the Mohawk. Numbers, however appalling, cannot convey the human anguish compressed into that 80-mile journey. Families that had come to clear and work their broad acres huddled with their few remaining animals in these crowded, make-shift fortifications, always in terror as they tried to plow and harvest.

Into this wounded land in the spring of 1781 returned Marinus Willett. He was, without exaggeration, its last hope, the indispensable man. If he could not protect the region, the frontier of New York could easily fall back to Schenectady. If that happened the resolute George Clinton would be governor of very little, and no part of his shrunken domain would be secure. The fate of much of this dimin-ished realm lay in Willett's hands: Clinton had charged him with the security of Albany, Tryon and Charlotte Counties.[61]

Willett brought his customary vigor and enthusiasm to his for-midable task, but the tools at his command were few and damaged. His regiment was to consist of new levies, induced to serve by the offer of bounty lands, since the currency offered little attraction. Willett soon found that all of the Charlotte County troops and some from Albany County refused to report because they sided with Vermont in its worsening dispute with New York State authority. (In addition to Governor Clinton's other pressures, he was facing the possibility of armed conflict with Vermont; much of General Gan-sevoort's time was occupied in watching this front.) Although some 1100 militia were enrolled in Tryon, Willett believed only about 500 were likely to turn out.[62]

Headquartered in Albany, where one of his brothers resided, Willett turned his immense energy toward forging the swords and shields of defense. In keeping with his temperament, he adopted an aggressive strategy: "It appears to me that nothing less can aliviate the present dread of the Inhabitants than a sickening reception of the Enemy should they again. . . visit these parts." He requested two or three cannon to give alarms and protested to the Governor that two of his soldiers had been imprisoned for debt: "To have a Soldier liable to be taken from their regiment and confined in Goal [jail] at a time when their Services are greatly wanted, without the Creditor having the least prospect of getting his money, is leaving it with power of disaffected persons materially to injure the Service."[63]

Next, he distributed his meager forces as best he could over his wide expanse of territory, stationing detachments at Saratoga, Ballston, German Flats, Canajoharie, Fort Hunter, Catskill, Johnstown and Schoharie; collectively they totaled less than 400 men.[64] These dispositions showed both the extent of Willett's responsibility and the paucity of his resources. On the exhausted frontier there were no ponderous, faceless legions in motion. Willett's position was closer to that of a modern youth soccer coach, but with a deadly twist. It is conceivable that he was personally acquainted with a large proportion of his troops. This part of the war had become finally an individual thing. In World War I, with armies being ground up, hardly anything less than the loss of a division attracted attention; on the Mohawk frontier of 1781 every man mattered, every loss was a tragedy.

Willett gave detailed instructions to his officers: "above all things guard against the disgrace of a surprise," he cautioned. He directed scouting parties to go out as far as "old Fort Schuyler" and, if possible, even to the Bay of Niaoure (present Sackets Harbor).[65] The reference to old Fort Schuyler probably meant the site in present Utica, but almost simultaneously the later Fort Schuyler (Fort Stanwix) was becoming a memory. After being severely damaged by flood and fire, it was abandoned in May 1781. Some American commanders suspected that the damage was not entirely accidental. Duty there had become even more hateful to the garrison; soldiers had to venture farther away for wood, and a party of 15 had been ambushed by Indians. Still, General Schuyler regretted the necessity: "If it had been possible to have sheltered the garrison. . . either in tents or huts I should have preferred it to an evacuation." He feared that "the Enemy will make it a temporary post as a receptacle to the disaffected, and it will inspire the Enemy and their Savage allies with fresh confidence and induce a belief that our cause is becoming desperate."[66]

No one was more aware of the importance of morale, and in one of the first entries in his regimental orderly book Willett issued an inspirational message:

> The greenness of the Troops and the importance of the service they are called to most powerfully point out the necessity of the greatest assiduity, vigilance and perseverance. The distresses of the Inhabitants we are called to protect demand every possible effort for their security. A cruel and barbarous Enemy that can't be too severely chastised ought to stimulate every officer and soldier to employ every possible exertion for their chastisement.[67]

It would take considerable time to shape these ragged forces into the instrument Willett desired, and he was not given the luxury of time. He had arrived near the beginning of the raiding season, and soon the enemy was upon him. In the type of warfare they conducted, the raiders enjoyed every advantage. They could choose their target and bring overwhelming power to the point of attack. The inhabitants, and the soldiers sent to defend them, could take cover—like rabbits, as Willett said—in their little forts. However, while cooped up there, the defenders would be unable to protect their houses, barns and crops. Nor could the state, which could scarcely provision its army, maintain a large number of refugees. This, obviously, was the goal of British strategy: to depopulate the frontier so it could no longer support the rebel war effort or provide a defense in depth for the heart of the state. Most of the raiders probably cared little about strategic considerations. Few Loyalists remained to be rescued, and there was little realistic hope of restoring the king's authority. The remaining inhabitants of the valley referred to the raiders as "destructives;" and indeed their main objective seemed to be to plunder and ruin.

Willett understood that if he were going to succeed he would have to exploit the attackers' few points of vulnerability. One was that they were far from their base, so that if pursued vigorously they would have no chance of relief or resupply. With their supporters gone, the raiders now thought of themselves as entering hostile country, and Burgoyne's experience weighed on their minds. "Bur-

NELSON GREENE
FORT PLAIN (IN THE MOHAWK VALLEY) NEW YORK
1944 AND 1946

goyned" had become a verb, and the attackers dreaded being captured by the people they had ravaged almost as much as the rebels feared being taken by Indians and subjected to prolonged torture. Another factor in Willett's favor was the Indians' dislike of sustained warfare. A final consideration was the psychological edge given by Willett's indomitable reputation—soon to be tested and confirmed.

Little more preparation could be done, and it was time for Willett to take the field. In May he went west to set up his headquarters. There is considerable confusion about the location of this command post, given variously as Canajoharie, Fort Plain and Fort Rensselaer. Fort Plain, now a separate community, was then considered to be part of the Canajoharie settlements. The fort, built in 1776, was officially named Fort Rensselaer, but the inhabitants disliked the name because it reminded them of the despised Robert Van Rensselaer, whose lack of vigor had disappointed them so grievously. Willett probably shared their contempt, but to avoid offending his superiors he felt compelled to continue using the official name.[68]

A new fort in the circle of outer defenses around Fort Plain was completed in the spring of 1781 on the farm of tories who had fled to Canada. According to tradition, when the colonel rode out to inspect the new stockade he was asked to name it. He replied, "Well, this is one of the nicest little forts on the frontier, and you may call it after me, if you please."[69] After the war neighbors removed the pickets they had contributed, and the fort was dismantled.[70]

Before settling in to his headquarters Willett toured the territory entrusted to him, venturing as far as German Flats. From there he dispatched letters to General Washington and Governor Clinton. The letter to Washington was longer because he described the region in considerable detail—information Clinton already knew well. In it

Overleaf: **Mohawk Valley historian and artist Nelson Greene drew on historic sources to create this depiction of Fort Plain at the time of General Washington's visit in the summer of 1783. The Fort Plain complex was then at its height in terms of number of structures. Colonel Willett probably lived in one of the houses in the foreground. Subsequent findings suggest that Greene was mistaken as to the location of some of the structures: for example, the large blockhouse in the center of the fort was probably situated where the eight-sided fortification is shown.** —Courtesy Fort Plain Museum

Willett revealed his deep sympathy for the sufferings of the inhabitants, as well as his conviction of the region's bright prospects:

> In such a country, blessed with so fine a soil, lying along a delightful river, which afforded an easy transportation of the produce to a valuable market, with a climate exceeded by none, it might have been expected a greater population [increase] would [have] taken place. But this was stagnated by means you are undoubtedly well acquainted with. These obstructions will I hope in a little time be removed and this part of the world—which is in itself one of the first places perhaps upon this Continent may expect to be surpassed by none. Flourish it must. Nothing but the hand of tyranny can prevent it much longer from becoming the garden of America.[71]

Willett estimated that only 800 of the 2500 militia on the rolls at the start of the war would now be available to respond. Of the missing two-thirds, "I don't think I shall give a very wild account if I say, that one third have been killed, or carried captive by the enemy; one third removed to the interior places of the country; and one third deserted to the enemy." Exclusive of the militia, he reported only 250 men available for duty. As he put it more bluntly to Clinton, "I am crowded with applications for guards, and have nothing to guard with."[72] Nevertheless, Willett did not succumb to the despair and inactivity that would have afflicted most men, and he vowed to Washington: "I can only promise to do everything in my power, for the relief of a people, of whom I had some knowledge in their prosperous days; and am now acquainted with in the time of their great distress; a people whose case I most sincerely commiserate."

While burdened with the multitudinous details of setting up a command in a devastated country, Willett gave considerable thought to his strategy. He planned to rotate his detachments through Fort Plain "so as to have an opportunity of acquainting myself as well as possible with every officer and soldier I may have in charge." He concluded that "the way to protect these parts is, in case the enemy should again appear this way with any thing of force, to collect all the strength we can get to a point, and endeavour to beat them in the field."[73]

Willett requested Washington's opinion of this approach, but before the commander could respond, Willett's concepts were given a direct test. Scouting reports, soon confirmed by the sight of smoke from burning settlements, told of a large enemy incursion. Putting his idea of immediate response into practice, Willett sent out messengers and scraped together as many men as he could find; altogether they totaled no more than 170. The invading force, led by a renegade named John Doxtader, consisted of Indians and loyalists; probably no British regulars were among them. They were at least as numerous as Willett's improvised legion and presumably more experienced.[74] Nevertheless, Willett was determined to give battle. He was a true man of action; his first impulse was to fight. In this respect he had changed not a bit since the day he had stepped forward to seize British munitions in New York. On the frontier, with its wild and often individualistic style of fighting, where boldness and resolution counted for more than elaborate planning, Willett was in his element.

Luckily, Willett's scouts had discovered the raiders' camp. On the assumption that they would return to the same place, Willett planned a night attack—a move so daring that even regular troops seldom attempted it. He headed south from Canajoharie, crossing the ridge that encloses the Mohawk River, into the present town of Sharon. Perhaps it was just as well that the scouts lost their way, so that Willett did not arrive until dawn. With the possibility of surprise lost, Willett faced difficult choices; the enemy had taken up a defensible position in a thick swamp, where a frontal attack would be foolhardy.

In woodland warfare elaborate battlefield maneuvers were out of the question. Only one tactic was manageable: the ambush, often preceded by a ruse. This was the method Willett employed. He detached part of his force as a reserve, then sent Lt. Jacob Sammons forward with ten men. Seeing them, the raiders burst out of their hiding places and dashed forward—directly into the fire of Willett's main force. At the height of the battle, Willett charged ahead. Waving his hat, he yelled, "The day is ours, boys, I can catch all the balls they can throw in my hat!" At this the enemy broke and ran, leaving on the battlefield nearly 40 dead and all the plunder they had taken. Willett lost five men, one of whom was the brave Capt. Robert McKean. In addition, at the start of the battle, Doxtader's Indians tied nine civilians they had captured to trees and tomahawked them.

Willett's attack, impulsive and impetuous, was characteristic. The image of him waving his hat as he charged sounds too theatrical to be true, yet it is in character. His reputation substituted for the artillery bombardment that would have preceded an assault in a

Above: The state marker for the Battle of Sharon Springs stands on the south side of Route 20 in the town of Sharon.

Below: The raiders probably camped in this cedar swamp, which may have changed little in the intervening time. Willett lured the enemy out of the swamp to fight on higher ground to the south, where the heaviest fighting probably took place beyond the state historical marker.

> *Abraham Ten Broeck Esquire Mayor of the City send greeting Know ye that in Testimony of the hi Conduct of Colonel Marinus Willet in the Action who with an inferior Force defeated and put to Frey, We do hereby admit and receive the said City. To have and to hold all the Rights Liber to the Freemen and Inhabitants of the said C public Seal of the said City to be affixed agree of July in the year of our Lord 1781.*

formal battle. Thereafter, sheer nerve and determination carried the day. It was also terribly risky. Willett was not only the soul of his army, but the backbone as well. If one of the bullets had caught him instead of the other way around, his little force would have disintegrated. The Continental Grand Army would have had a better chance of continuing without Washington than the Mohawk Valley defenders without Willett.

This clash, known as the Battle of Sharon, or Sharon Springs, made Willett again a hero. The grateful burghers of Albany voted him the freedom of the city. The colonel, characteristically, thanked his men profusely for their courageous performance. The Indians, for whom the spiritual world was not separated from daily reality, now referred to Willett as "The Devil," and this awe became a tangible factor.[75] The fight in the cedar swamp was virtually the first incident in two years that had raised the morale of the embattled frontier, and as such it was a turning point. Still, it did not bring an end to the valley's torment. Smaller raiding parties continued their depredations, scalping, burning, carrying families into captivity. Even Willett's hasty mobilization could not overtake these fleet bands.

any To all to whom these Presents shall come
se this Board entertain of Bravery & military
tenth Instant near Turlough in Tryon County
the Enemy under the Command of Brant &
inus Willet a Freeman and Citizen of the said
eeoms and Franchises whatsoever belonging
Witness whereof we have hereunto caused the
a Resolution of Common Council this 19 d
Wm. Ten Broeck   Mayor

Courtesy New York State Library

Willett's sense of personal responsibility for the security of the Mohawk Valley, combined with his constant awareness of the inadequate resources at his command, led to frequent outbursts of frustration. Only a few days after his success, which he had the wisdom to regard as "greater than we had a right to hope for," the colonel expressed concern about a colony of "Rascally disaffected Inhabitants" which had gathered at Torloch (or Dorloch). Infuriated by the "long train of horrid Villiany" of these "Miscreant Inhabitants," Willett concluded that "nothing short of a gallows can be a just reward for their actions."[76]

On one level this letter highlighted the uncertain and shifting loyalties of the troubled region, but Willett was in no position to take such a detached view and actually requested Governor Clinton's permission to carry out wholesale hangings. The governor must have been alarmed by this proposal from the fiery colonel, for he replied almost immediately. Clinton had no greater regard for tories and renegades than did Willett, but his service as governor had instilled a

respect for proper legal procedures. While conceding that the Torloch renegades were "undoubtedly guilty of high Treason of the
blackest Hue," they were not subject to martial law and thus must
be dealt with "by the Ordinary Courts of Justice." After recording
this necessary disclaimer, Clinton then vented his true feelings,
exclaiming "What a pitty it is they had not fallen when in Arms ag't
us. . . ."[77]

Through the weary summer of 1781 Willett struggled to make
the most of an impossible situation. Supplies of food and equipment
were chronically insufficient. The militia were deficient in numbers
and training. Small but damaging raids went unpunished. Testifying
to the exhaustion of New York, Massachusetts troops were requested
for service on the Mohawk frontier, but even they were delayed in
arriving. Governor Clinton faced the additional burden of the rebel-
lious Vermonters, who were reportedly negotiating with the British.
In an odd turn of events, these contacts were conducted by Col. Barry
St. Leger, who was adding another chapter to his disappointing career
while in command of a force on Lake Champlain.

By September Willett, while declaring his willingness to persist,
confessed that "to serve another Campaign with the embarasments
that has hitherto and is like to continue to attend this—I hope will
never fall to my lott again."[78] Yet even while absorbed in his duties
on the frontier, part of Willett's mind lingered elsewhere. When word
came of a French victory over a British fleet off the Virginia capes,
Willett's immediate reaction was "May it pave the way for our speedy
entrance into the long lost Metropolis of this State."[79] The man who
had built a reputation as a frontier fighter and whom the Indians
regarded as a devil remained at heart a city boy.

Several days after the battle of Sharon, but without having
learned of it, General Washington responded favorably to Willett's
letter of July 6: "The dispositions which you are making for the
defence of the Country upon the Mohawk River appear to me
judicious, as I have ever been of opinion that small stationary Garrisons were of no real utility. By having your parties constantly in
motion and ready to unite upon occasion, the small parties of the
Enemy will be checked and their Main Body may be suddenly
attacked, if they commit themselves too far into the settlements."[80]

Washington's endorsement only added to the frustration Willett
felt at not being able to carry out his policy, but late in the season he

was given the opportunity he sought. Down the usual invasion route from Buck's (later Carleton) Island and Oswego came a sizable incursion led by Major John Ross, accompanied by the dread Walter Butler. Unlike Doxtader's band, this force contained a large proportion of British regulars and relatively few Indians. In his later report Willett described them as "a fine Detachment of Troops [sent] upon such a Paltry Business."[81] Perhaps, as historian Howard Swiggett suggests, they were meant to be one element of a larger strategy.[82]

After leaving their boats at Oneida Lake, Ross achieved complete surprise; despite its size his force was not detected until it appeared far down the valley on October 24. Reports of enemy activity to the northward, around Saratoga and Lake Champlain, had turned American attention in that direction; Willett's elaborate scouting system had failed. Repeating the course of Johnson's raid the year before, Ross began devastating one of the few unscathed sections of the valley. He approached within 12 miles of Schenectady, but then the fear of being surrounded began to press on him. Indeed, Willett, though caught by surprise, was dashing around gathering troops. Ross retreated to the familiar surroundings of Johnson Hall, and Willett overtook him there October 25.

Marinus Willett was now about to fight the most important battle of his career. The British had played into his hands by giving him the kind of open battle he had sought. Once again he was outnumbered: estimates of Ross's army ranged from 400 to more than 1000; Willett's figure of around 600 is probably the most reliable. Against them, Willett was able to muster about 400; presumably they were also inferior in quality. Once again, skill and determination would be critical. An all-out frontal assault seemed foolhardy; so Willett divided his force, sending Maj. Aaron Rowley of Massachusetts with about 60 men from that state and New York around to the left. This violated the conventional prohibition against dividing one's force in the face of the enemy, but generals such as Robert E. Lee have used the method with success. Willett posted his one artillery piece on the right and attacked from that direction.

The battle seemed to be going well when suddenly one of those inexplicable panics that are the dread of all militia commanders seized Willett's men. They broke and ran in disorder toward the village. Now Willett made a brilliant decision; instead of trying to stop the rout and possibly sacrificing his life in the process, he and his officers fell back to the village and worked desperately to reassemble their shattered battalion. It was late in the afternoon of a gloomy October day. They heard renewed firing, and Willett knew that Major Rowley was making the attack that, under the original plan, was supposed to finish off the enemy. Instead, Rowley risked being annihilated once the British realized how small his detachment really was.

The gallant Rowley, already wounded, was in danger of suffering the fate of Colonel Brown. Under these circumstances, Robert Van Rensselaer would have gone home for dinner; but Willett was formed in a different mold. Gathering as many troops as he could, he returned to the fray and recovered the lost cannon. Ross might still have got the better of it, but darkness was falling. The fear of being "burgoyned" was upon him, and he began a retreat, leaving Willett in possession of the field. As a result, the Americans were able to capture about 50 of the enemy, mostly wounded. At first it was reported that each side had lost about 40 killed, but the actual totals were probably lower.[83]

There is no doubt Willett had been mauled, so that it took time to regroup; but he was not ready to lose an opportunity to crush the invaders. He reassembled his force at German Flats. After a day it became apparent that Ross was not returning by way of Oneida Lake but was making a perilous overland retreat along a faint trail to Oswego. With characteristic initiative, Willett saw a chance to intercept them. He selected nearly 500 of his fittest men, including 60 Oneidas who had volunteered to join him, and gave them provisions for five days. Willett promised each of the Oneidas a blanket as an incentive to "exert themselves to overtake the enemy." (On his return the colonel found "it was not in my power to comply with the promise I had made in behalf of the public," and more than ten years later he was still pleading with the state to furnish the blankets.)[84]

On the 28th Willett began his pursuit, marching through an early snowstorm, and on the next day, the fourth after the clash at Johnstown, his scouts located the enemy. By then the invaders were in full flight through an endless, dismal forest, the wet snow further dampening their spirits. Though exhausted and hungry, they had discarded most of their packs and were moving "in an Indian file upon a constant trott, and one man's being Knocked in the head or falling off into the woods never stoped the Progress of his Neighbour."[85] Despite all Willett's efforts, he could not overtake the fleeing raiders. His best chance came at West Canada Creek, where Ross's men had to ford a sometimes turbulent stream. A detachment fought a rear-guard action there, and when they continued their flight the Americans who crossed the creek found the body of Walter Butler lying on the stony shore. A captain's commission was taken from his pocket, perhaps the same he had flaunted in 1777 when he was sentenced to death at the trial at which Willett presided. The judgment that had been rendered that day had finally been carried out.[86]

No one can be sure of the exact site of the clash in which Walter Butler was killed, but this spot on West Canada Creek is probably close. The photo was taken on nearly the same date as the battle, and the creek is not affected at this point by the dam that forms Hinckley Reservoir, so the flow of water may be similar.

So much was the mysterious Walter Butler a figure of dark romance that numerous legends arose as to the manner of his death. Almost certainly he was slain by one of the Oneidas. Butler was vilified as the source of the atrocities and suffering inflicted on the Northern Frontier, and the settlers rejoiced at the news of his death. Word of the climactic victory at Yorktown reached the area at nearly the same time, but it was said that the inhabitants of the Mohawk took more pleasure in the death of young Butler. Their feelings were understandable: General Washington's fundamental decision to concentrate his limited resources in the main army while leaving the frontier to fend for itself—except for the Sullivan-Clinton expedition—had created a situation in which two parallel wars were raging. The weary and battered settlers had surely earned whatever respite Colonel Willett won for them.

As at Sharon Springs, Willett had the good sense not to attempt a headlong pursuit, which could have subjected his men to the same hardship and dispersal as the fleeing enemy. In a memorable phrase, he reported that "to the Compassion of a starving Wilderness, we left them in a fair way of Receiving a Punishment better suited to their Merit than a musquet ball, a Tomahawk or Captivity."[87] Actual British casualties are not certain; probably most of them made it back to their base, though in a famished and exhausted condition.[88]

Once again Willett had gained the military glory he craved. Maj. Gen. Stirling, commanding the Northern Department, concluded that Willett "through this whole affair seems to have acted the part of a Vigilant, prudent, experienc'd Officer, & altho the Enemy finally evaded his pursuit, his Conduct was such as must reflect the highest honor upon his Military Character."[89] Willett himself did not exaggerate his exploit. He wrote that "tho. I think the affair might have turned out better, yet it is a most Capital stroke in favour of the County of Tryon." Well aware what a near thing it had been, he was copious in his praise of his men, singling out Major Rowley for special commendation. With good reason and characteristic bluntness he complained of the injury he had suffered when Gen. John Stark had called away two companies of troops from Johnstown: "such an Addition to our strength at Johnstown must have assured us a most Compleat victory at that Place and the Calling of those Troops from this Quarter to a part w[h]ere they have the whole Eastern world at hand to Reinforce them, appeared to me as unaccountable at that time as it has Proved Injurious since."[90]

Textbooks tell us that fighting virtually ceased after Yorktown, creating a strange truce that lasted until peace was concluded a year and a half later. In most of the country this was true, but war on New York's Northern Frontier had its own reasons. After spending the winter in Albany, with occasional visits to his outposts, Willett

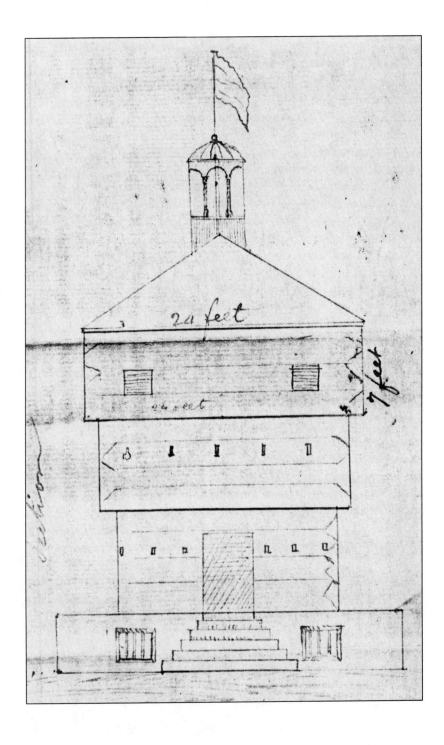

returned to his command at Fort Plain as the 1782 campaign season opened.

Governor Clinton had begged him to continue, and Willett accepted after putting various personal concerns on the record. The fact that he held only a state commission still troubled him, as it created the humiliating possibility that he could be outranked and possibly commanded by former junior officers who had Continental rank. He was also miffed and resentful over missing an opportunity to purchase state lands and in a moment of pique wrote Clinton "to serve another campaign under such disadvantages as I did the last, and to come home in the winter and sit down with empty pockets is what I cannot find a Dissposition to Comply with. . . ." He was careful to add, however, "The restoring to me. . . my former Rank. . . with the prospect of receiving such pay as would free me from my present difficulties would make the Command your Excellency desires to keep me in very pleasing to me."[91] It does not appear that this was done, but Willett was a soldier above all, and in the end he buckled on his sword and went back to his post in the Mohawk Valley, a post that only he could fill.

Bolstered by several companies of New Hampshire troops, Willett probably was in a stronger position than in 1781. Recruitment of New York state troops seems to have gone reasonably well. Willett's experience had given him realistic ideas about recruiting. He knew better than to expect soldiers to me inspired by the patriotism and hostility to the British that motivated him. "Money and Clothing are in my Opinion the best means of procuring Soldiers. Hence I conclude something that will make a Show as a Bounty and a Suit of good Cloaths ready to Deliver each Recruit upon his entering into the service," would be most effective. "Land with speculations in Land may do something, but I do not understand that business," he added.[92]

Willett's reputation and the growing unwillingness of the British to subsidize large attacks gave the Northern Frontier some relief. However, the memory of living in constant dread, with ruthless

Facing page: **Original drawing for the blockhouse at Fort Plain designed by the French engineer Villefranche. This drawing was not known to Nelson Greene when he attempted to represent the structure in his rendering of Fort Plain.** --Courtesy American Antiquarian Society

enemies possibly lurking in every woodland edge, did not fade quickly. Those of us who step out of our houses at night or go off to work without imagining danger can never understand. Harvest was a time of terror, and a year's labor could be destroyed in hours by "destructives." Farmers took their weapons into the fields, working under guard; mills and storehouses were guarded. In the fifth year after Oriskany, anxious farmers continued to beg for protection. One remarkable petition came to Colonel Willett from the Palatine district:

> [Your petitioners] lay expost to the enemy they have destroyed the lives of a great many of the Inhapitends Carried others into captivity demolished and burned down many settlemends and villages and blundered the property of the Inhapitends of the same to our very great distress and Impoverishment. . .
>
> we hope your honour will take this in consiteration and give us about one hundred men in fort house and fort Wolrath and George Klock his Blockhouse near the christmill and fort Zimerman and at George G. Klocks then we shall be able to keep a schout out and if the enemy should be discovered with their small parties we shall be able to pursue them imetiatly before they two any damage on our frontiers if we gand no assistance we want to be able to remain on our hapitations the enemy is daily about us and kill and schulp our prothers and trive of our chattle. . . .[93]

Beneath the superficially comical aspect caused by giving German sound values to English letters, this petition represents a pathetic cry for help from people who had been subjected to years of violence and insecurity. But how was Colonel Willett, who had perhaps 400 men spread across his vast command, going to fill additional garrisons?

Nevertheless, Willett could take considerable satisfaction from the 1782 campaign season. It had not been a brilliant year on the Northern Frontier, but there had been no major invasions and battles. Despite the pervasive fear that hung over the valley, the crops had been brought in. As he mustered out most of his troops and rode back to Albany in the gathering chill of November, he had reason to be pleased with his accomplishments. Marinus Willett is widely celebrated as the "hero of Fort Stanwix," but it is likely that he performed a greater, if less recognized, service in saving the Mohawk Valley. Of necessity, American commanders had to fight under

conditions of extreme deprivation, but few had done more with
skimpier resources.

* * *

It is not certain whether Mary Willett had joined her husband in
Albany the previous winter, and as 1782 closed the colonel hoped to
pass a quiet time with her in new quarters he had built at Fort Plain.
Soon after joining her at Fishkill, Willett took advantage of the
location to talk with General Washington, who was camped with the
main army across the Hudson at Newburgh. This visit drastically
changed the colonel's plans for a winter of domestic tranquility.

The commander-in-chief knew that the prospects for peace appeared promising, and already he was looking ahead to peacetime
problems. With his longstanding interest in western lands, he had
reason to be concerned that the British would not yield their frontier
posts, holding them to block America's westward expansion. If he
could seize any of these posts before hostilities ended, it would leave
one less obstacle to trouble the new nation. Faraway posts such as
Niagara, Detroit and Carleton Island were effectively beyond his
reach, but Fort Ontario, the main British base at Oswego, might be
accessible.[94] The British had alarmed Washington by reoccupying and
repairing the fort in 1782. Now the arrival of Willett, with his renown
as a frontier fighter and master of the bold stroke, formed a combination that made an attack on the threatening outpost irresistibly
tempting.

For Colonel Willett the prospect was also irresistible. It was
inconceivable for him to turn down a request from a man he idolized
or reject a chance to earn glory against a hated enemy. Without
hesitation he accepted command of the Oswego expedition, yet even
the intrepid colonel acknowledged that warfare had lost some of its
appeal: "This was the first time that an opening ever presented itself
to Col. Willett of a chance of procuring fame, that his heart did not
vibrate with joy."[95]

A rapid, frequent and highly secure correspondence soon began
between Willett and Washington, who wrote in his own hand. So
enthusiastic was Washington that he even considered journeying by
sleigh to Fort Herkimer or Fort Plain to see the expedition off.[96] Due
in part to a lack of medical supplies, the commander stressed that

only a surprise attack would be acceptable. Plans for a midwinter raid strained America's support system. A nation that could scarcely meet the ordinary needs of its troops now had to provide large numbers of sleds, snowshoes and gloves. Willett resorted to irregular means of impressing sleighs and, fearing civil prosecution, asked Washington to backdate a warrant.[97]

Careful planning was absolutely essential. An almanac indicated that February 11 was the ideal date for the attack. On that day a waxing moon would provide light for the approach to the fort but would set just in time for a predawn assault to take place under cover of darkness. With as little advance notice as possible, Willett assembled his troops at Fort Herkimer on February 8. He mustered perhaps 400 to 500 men—exact numbers were not given—consisting of picked members of his levies and part of a Rhode Island black regiment. Participation of these Rhode Island troops was unusual, since it was commonly assumed that African-Americans were not well suited for service under conditions of extreme cold.

On the ninth Willett's expedition crossed Oneida Lake. They left their sleighs behind, as they had become a hinderance to rapid movement.[98] At the close of the next day the force had reached Oswego Falls (present Fulton). There they halted to build ladders—constructing them earlier would have been cumbersome and would have revealed the purpose of the expedition. Willett's scouts had advised that the walls of Fort Ontario towered 30 feet above a ditch nine feet deep, with a row of pickets in the center of the ditch. Willett proposed to lay boards from the glacis to these pickets and place ladders from there to the parapet so that ladders 14 feet long would be sufficient.[99] This was a risky plan, but the prospect of constructing 30-foot ladders and maneuvering them through dark woods seemed more unattractive.[100]

There was an odd circularity to Willett's military career: as he had returned to Lake Champlain and to Fort Stanwix, he now approached Oswego, which he had last seen almost 25 years earlier. Following the Oswego River, Willett's expedition was four miles from the fort by ten or eleven o'clock at night, leaving four hours before moonset would provide cover. At this point the ice on the river became unreliable, forcing the party to proceed overland. Willett gave final detailed instructions to his officers. Then, instead of following the river bank, he took the advice of his Indian guide, who said he knew a shorter route cross-country. The prize, as Willett later wrote, seemed within easy grasp.

That moment, when, as Willett wrote later, "my breast was full of ardor and the most animated determination," proved to be the high point of his expedition. Thereafter, prospects sank with sickening rapidity. After two hours of laborious marching through swamps and woods covered with heavy snow, encumbered by the clumsy ladders, had not brought the fort into view, Willett became concerned. He was already near the head of the column, and he soon overtook the guide, an Oneida named Captain John, who also held a Continental commission. The colonel's worst fears were confirmed: they were lost. Willett at first suspected treachery; he had tried to guard against that by promising Captain John that he would not have to participate in the actual storming of the fort. Though Willett put the scout under guard as a precaution, he concluded that Captain John had gone astray by following snowshoe tracks which he mistakenly believed would lead to the fort.[101]

When the exhausted soldiers finally glimpsed their objective it was in the pale, unpromising light of a February dawn. Washington had admonished Willett, "If you do not succeed by Surprise the attempt will be unwarrantable." With the possibility of surprise lost, there was no choice but to retreat. Willett had approached this mission with his usual complete confidence. Thus he expected to provision his men in captured Fort Ontario and had not brought food and clothing sufficient for an unsuccessful return. The homeward journey by already weary men over a frozen landscape of woods and swamps turned into one of the legendary ordeals of the war. Failure made the weight of cold seem heavier; even Willett admitted that once the prospect of success vanished in the dawn, "great fatigue got the better of the spirits of the soldiers."[102] Two men, one Rhode Islander and one Yorker, were left behind in the snow. Many others were lamed by frostbite, and dozens made it only because they were dragged or carried by their comrades.

Soon after the numbed warriors staggered back to Fort Herkimer they learned that a provisional peace had been signed. Willett had failed in the last mission of the war, a defeat all the more disappointing because of the intense interest of his commander. Not long after his return, Willett sat down and composed a painful letter to Washington. With his usual gush of words, he recounted the details of his expedition and recited the reasons why it had gone awry. Then he had to confront the stark reality, and from the anguish of his soul blurted out "Yet I have unfortunately failed."[103] It never occurred to Willett that the attack itself, which depended on a large number of circumstances going precisely right, might have failed. Nineteenth century historian Jeptha Simms later spoke to Americans who had been prisoners inside the fort, and they told him that the strength of the fort would have meant almost certain disaster for an attack.[104]

Washington responded a few days later. With characteristic magnanimity, he reassured Willett that "I am happy in the persuasion that no Imputation or reflection can justly reach your Character, and that you are enabled to derive much Consolation from the animated Zeal, fortitude and Activity of the Officers and Soldiers who accompanied you." A man who until the final redeeming triumph at Yorktown had borne his full share of disappointment, Washington surely wrote from the heart when he told Willett "The failure, it seems, must be attributed to some of those unaccountable Events, which are not within the controul of human Means and which, tho' they often occur in military life, yet require not only the fortitude of the Soldier, but the calm reflection of the Philosopher, to bear."[105]

Fortunately, the discouraging withdrawal from Oswego was not the final episode of Marinus Willett's war. The dreary February expedition represented the somber, oppressive North Country winter, but brighter days lay ahead. The king's pronouncement of peace inspired celebrations that were richly deserved, and Willett participated in one at Albany. But there remained a long, wearing interlude before final arrangements were ratified, during which the exhausted United States had to maintain a credible military force. Fidgety during what he called "this irksome interval," Washington decided to improve the time by taking an extensive trip to parts of New York State he had never seen. When he expressed the desire "to reconnoitre those places, where the remarkable posts were established, and the ground which became famous by being the theatre of action in 1777," he became perhaps the first heritage tourist.[106]

After traveling north as far as Crown Point and viewing the already legendary battlefields of Ticonderoga and Saratoga, Washington returned to Schenectady and prepared for the western leg of his journey. Willett was still in command of the valley and during that period seemed to be spending much of his time at Fort Herkimer.

Washington's excursion, during which he produced little official correspondence, is not as well documented as most of his wartime career. There is uncertainty as to his whereabouts on a given day and who accompanied him. Apparently there is no confirmation that Willett joined his commander, but it is reasonable to accept valley historian Nelson Greene's conclusion that "he doubtless accompanied Washington to Fort Stanwix and Oriskany in order to tell the military chieftain something of the famous siege and battle."[107] Governor Clinton was a member of Washington's party, and it is unimaginable that Willett would have missed a chance for leisurely conversation with these men. What immense relief and satisfaction they must have felt on that ride through their newly-free land! All the hardships they had endured in eight years of uncertain struggle made the triumph won by their supreme fortitude sweeter.

General Washington remained concerned about the western posts. Under the terms of peace the western boundary of the United States was to be the Mississippi, but the commander-in-chief was fearful that the British would either fail to hand over their outposts or depart so precipitately that the forts would be damaged before the Americans could take control. Washington's recent familiarity with the region now paid dividends. He directed Colonel Willett to improve the roads and waterways to Oneida Lake so that troops and supplies could be moved quickly to Oswego and Niagara.[108] He also spoke of building blockhouses at the Oneida Carry and later mentioned erecting buildings at Fort Stanwix, indicating he contemplated a partial reoccupation of the fort.[109]

Washington was so hopeful that he had troops ready to move westward. Instead, he suffered one of his last disappointments of the war, as the British commander in Canada refused to yield the posts. Perhaps hoping that the United States would disintegrate and seeking to retain influence with the Indians, the British held the bases more than ten years longer. Colonel Willett at least had the satisfaction of knowing that Washington's confidence in him had not been diminished by the Oswego venture.

The long delay in finalizing peace arrangements drained the event of much of its joy. Discord and confusion prevailed, heightened by the emptiness of state and federal treasuries. Still, there was magnificent elation on Evacuation Day, November 25, 1783, when the British finally departed New York City. Americans in serviceworn uniforms marched in almost on the heels of the British regulars, still brilliant in scarlet coats and burnished arms, but vanquished.

Colonel Willett's activities during this period of transition are largely unrecorded. On October 3 he wrote Washington to inquire whether he should keep his troops on duty, but the general, in his reply of the 16th, was unable to provide definite orders.[110] By then many Continentals had disbanded, and Willett's levies may have followed before Winter set in. Without a ceremonial closure, and often without pay, the men took their muskets and dispersed to their scattered homes. It was probably only in later years that they came to understand the magnitude of what they had achieved.

On November 27 Governor Clinton named Willett and another colonel to take charge of houses and lands that had been abandoned by loyalists.[111] Once again, Clinton had found the right man for the job. The two colonels' responsibilities covered the entire state, so it is not clear when Willett returned to New York City. The colonels were authorized to use abandoned properties to house people who had fled the British invasion of 1776 and now lacked habitation. Willett himself was in that category: there had been fires in the city under British occupation, and it is not known whether the colonel's former residence survived or where he and Mary lived on their return. For them the passage from wartime to peacetime was not as sharp as for most others, but at some point of finality the realization must have come to Willett that the war and the fame it had brought him were over. The Son of Liberty was now able to enjoy the freedom for which he had risked his life on countless occasions.

**Plaque honoring Marinus Willett in
Washington Park, Albany.**

V. ECHOES OF THE DRUMS

Thus he lived, growing old amidst the esteem and affections of his fellow-citizens; and as time continually diminished the number of his old associates in arms, becoming like one of a few noble trees of a once large and flourishing forest, more and more an object of respect and veneration. —Narrative of the Military Actions of Colonel Marinus Willett.

MARINUS WILLETT, deservedly regarded as a hero of independence, was 43 when the war ended. More than half his life remained, but although it was an active and prominent life, the public portion was often unsatisfactory. The boldness and clarity of purpose he had displayed in his military career seemed to find no ready outlet in civilian life. A stream that had flowed with power and directness in the rugged hills had trouble finding the proper channel through the peaceful lowlands.

In his political career, Willett was accused of being wavering or erratic. Perhaps a more accurate appraisal is that he was consistent in his principles but uncertain how to apply them. For many years he followed Aaron Burr and was one of those friends who "loaned" Burr money to support his reckless lifestyle.[112] When that brilliant but variable star faded after killing Alexander Hamilton in their famous duel, Willett was tainted by association.

In contrast to Willett's voluminous wartime writings, no elaboration of his political ideas seems to survive. Judging by his actions, he saw the wealthy Federalists who took charge after the war as little more than another version of the oligarchy that had dominated the colony under British rule. Before the war he had observed the wealthy aristocratic DeLanceys battling the wealthy aristocratic Livingstons, with little gain to the common man whatever the outcome.

Still and forever the loyal Son of Liberty, Willett opposed the new lords as he had the old. Thus he alined with George Clinton as an anti-Federalist in the belief that a strong central government would give the new aristocracy even more power and become a greater threat to individual liberty. In the first postwar elections, Willett and other former Sons of Liberty were elected to the state legislature. This was the flush of victory and also the high point of the Sons' influence. Soon afterward, conservative forces reasserted themselves; and the former radicals waned, although a line of descent can be traced from the Sons of Liberty to Tammany Hall.

Willett never actually served in the legislature. In a way this is regrettable, as an opportunity for fiery oratory was lost. Possibly this is one of the considerations Governor Clinton had in mind when he instead gave the colonel an appointment as sheriff of New York City. This was a lucrative and important post, but it highlighted the contradiction in Willett's character between the rowdy populist and the strict disciplinarian. Willett was now charged with suppressing the kind of riotous behavior he had formerly instigated.

The contrast was brought out keenly during the so-called Shays' Rebellion of late 1786 and early 1787, when impoverished yeomen in Massachusetts took up arms to keep their farms from being confiscated for debt. After being dispersed in their home state, many took refuge in New York and raided across the border. Massachusetts governor James Bowdoin, who had raised a merchant army to crush the rebels, asked Governor Clinton for help. Clinton took Willett as sort of a military adviser when he met with Gen. Benjamin Lincoln, who had commanded the Massachusetts forces with conspicuously more success than he had achieved against the British during the war.

For Clinton and Willett the situation presented awkward choices. Politically and temperamentally they might have had reason to support the tattered farmers. Many of them were the same kind of men—perhaps the very same individuals—who as militiamen had been sent to Willett's aid in the Mohawk Valley. Yet Clinton was trapped in a dilemma: if he did not help another state cope with internal disorder, he would be strengthening the case for a strong central government. Willett, in turn, was charged with upholding the law. Clinton and Willett met with General Lincoln on March 17, 1787; and the governor's decisive instructions to civil and militia leaders persuaded the insurgents to depart.[113]

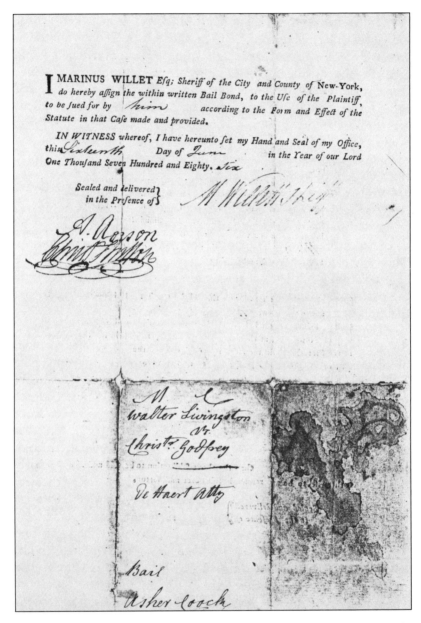

**Typical document bearing Willett's signature as sheriff of New York.
The A. Aorson who signed as witness may be Aaron Aorson, formerly
a captain in the Third New York regiment.** —Courtesy Fort Stanwix National
Monument.

Willett resigned as sheriff in 1788 to help Clinton fight the proposed United States Constitution. In his customary florid style, he described the result of the Philadelphia convention as "a Monster with open mouth and monstrous Teeth ready to devour all before it," and "an extraordinary conception" that totally departed from the principles of the Revolution.[114] As candidates from New York City to a state convention, Willett and the other anti-federalists were crushed. Despite this defeat, Willett remained true to his convictions, and as late as 1790 he and others of like mind were still trying to repeal or amend the hated covenant.[115] In contrast, Peter Gansevoort, true to his origins, supported the Constitution.

In his home city the war hero Marinus Willett belonged to a seemingly permanent political minority. Only during brief cracks in the opposition front was he able to garner anything for himself. The most noted example was when he edged into the New York City mayoralty (then an appointive position) for nine months in 1807-1808.

George Clinton's staunchest efforts were unable to halt the momentum to approve the Constitution in New York. Despite this defeat, he held on as governor, and as such was able to appoint Willett to another term as sheriff in 1791. Although he remained consistent to the political views he had held before the war, paradoxically Willett's economic position had changed drastically. As a Son of Liberty he had possessed little property and no real financial security. In peacetime, as a result of his association with Governor Clinton, his position as sheriff, and state grants to officers, he became a substantial landowner. He acquired thousands of acres in different sections of upstate New York. Considering that he claimed to know nothing of land speculation in 1781, he had progressed rapidly.

Upstate, Willett could have lived like a squire, and in the years just after the war the populace, who remembered him as the indispensable man, surely would have granted him any political office within their power. Instead, he remained a city man, and therefore consigned himself to being a political outsider. Of all his properties the one that mattered most to him personally was part of the former DeLancey property on the east side of Manhattan. This confiscated estate was an attractive speculation, but for the colonel also the site for a home.

According to Thomas Jones, Willett acquired several tracts of DeLancey's forfeited estate at a total cost of 5500 New York pounds, or over $18,000.[116] Another study shows Willett (with John Lamb) purchasing only one tract, the block bounded by Grand, Sheriff, Broome and Willett Streets.[117] Two of these streets—Willett obviously, but also Sheriff—are supposedly named for the colonel.[118]

Marinus Willett's residence.

In the vicinity of Corlears Hook, a prominent bulge of Manhattan into the East River, Willett built Cedar Grove, a mansion that testified to his new status in society. Here he gave Mary the home she had craved during her years of stressful exile. Mary Willett did not enjoy these surroundings for long, as she died in July 1793. More than a year later there also died at Cedar Grove Marinus's father Edward, at the age of 92. The venerable loyalist had probably never accepted American independence, but he had become reconciled with his patriot son.

It is possible that father and son had never been as estranged as is supposed. In a letter written during the Canadian campaign of 1775,

Marinus admonished his son, "Let your Honored Grand Father &
Mother those Dr parents of mine know of my wellfare when ever
you hear from me."[119] However the British conquest of New York
City a few months later, which made refugees of the colonel and his
wife, while Edward Willett continued living on Long Island under
British protection, forced a physical if not an emotional separation
of father and son.

Some sources state that the colonel and Mary were divorced at
the time of her death, but there seems to be no documentary
confirmation. On the contrary, she apparently died in Willett's home
and was described as his wife. More tellingly, he did not remarry until
after her death. During the war he had always been deeply solicitous
toward her, knowing the anguish she had endured and the inability
to find release in action, as he could. He always seemed eager to spend
time with her whenever his military duty allowed; she even visited
him at Fort Stanwix early in 1778. If there was an estrangement, it
must have occurred after the war.

One factor that could have brought about a separation is a scandal
connecting Marinus and a Mrs. Elizabeth Seeber while the colonel
was in command at Fort Plain. According to an account in Jeptha
Simms' *Frontiersmen of New York*[120], Mrs. Seeber was what would
later be called a "grass widow." Her husband, Henry, belonged to a
respected family, but his fondness for the jug had alienated his wife
so that they were not living together. Colonel Willett was undeniably
an attractive and commanding figure, and under the severe strains of
frontier warfare a relationship developed that in time produced a son,
who was named Marinus Willett Seeber. Simms further relates that
the colonel accepted responsibility for the child and provided for his
care and education. When grown to manhood the young fellow
returned to his birthplace but was rejected by members of the Seeber
family and forced to leave. After that, he disappears from the historical record.

Simms began collecting stories of the border wars when many of
the participants were still living. The account of Willett's illegitimate
son, for example, was attributed to a member of the Seeber family.[121]
Simms used the vacuum cleaner approach to history, swallowing
anything that presented itself without much sorting. The Willett
scandal is more fully described than some of his other narratives, but
was not supported by other documentation, and by its nature perhaps

could not be. (The many later repetitions all derive from Simms' account.)

Liaisons of this sort were routine on the frontier, and one can hardly blame the participants for seeking a fleeting comfort amid the danger and brutality of partisan warfare. It is noteworthy, however, that, in addition to the lack of corroborating evidence, this is the only such scandal that tarnishes Willett's name. Moreover, such a lapse would be out of character for Willett who, unlike many of his fellow officers, was a man of genuine religious conviction. Although it is hardly unprecedented for righteous people to succumb to temptation, one should not ignore the deep strain of morality and religious rectitude that appears so regularly in Willett's correspondence.

Barely three months after Mary's death, Willett married a widow, Susannah Vardill (or Vardle). This alliance was genuinely a disaster, and a bill of divorce was filed November 11, 1799, although the decree did not become final until 1805. Within a few months after the filing, Willett furnished New York gossips a topic that must have sustained them for an entire season when he married a woman more than thirty years younger, Margaret Bancker (1774-1867). By the time the earlier divorce became final in 1805, Willett had demonstrated his vitality by fathering three children. His last child was born in 1808, when the frontier warrior was 68.

This third marriage seems to have been successful despite the age difference and granted the colonel belated satisfaction. His four sons all bore Marinus as a first or middle name (the sole daughter escaped this blessing and took her mother's name). What at first may seem like a distasteful display of egotism is capable of another, more touching, explanation. These late children were probably named at least as much in memory of the colonel's lost but unforgotten first son as in honor of their father. Indeed, these nineteenth century boys fulfilled the expectations Marinus Willett had held for his lost son, and by then the old veteran was able to provide them advantages that were nearly beyond his means when his first son was growing up. (In a heartfelt letter to Marinus, Jr., written soon after arriving at Fort Stanwix in 1777, Willett affirmed that "My eye is wholly fixed upon your Advantages of Improvement" and promised make whatever sacrifices were needed—"to shorten my own coat if it is necessary.")[122]

The firstborn of Willett's later family actually became a doctor, though he died before his 40th birthday. Another became a minister and another, who carried on the name of Edward Willett, was a lawyer. Two of these sons extended the family trait of longevity by surviving into the 1890s. Thus, two generations spanned nearly 160 years; a child of a man born in 1740 lived to the threshold of the twentieth century.[123]

The most satisfying parts of Willett's public life after 1783 were those that had some military aspect. He was one of the original members of the New York chapter of the Society of the Cincinnati, an organization restricted to officers of the War for Independence and their eldest male progeny. In a country with democratic pretensions, this society was accused by its political enemies of forming a hereditary aristocracy. By joining, Willett again put his military loyalty and associations ahead of the opinions of his political allies. Willett never served as an officer of the Society, though he was an active member of the club that included many of his wartime comrades, but also his nemesis deRoussy.[124]

In 1790 Willett was asked by President Washington and War Secretary Henry Knox to undertake a peace mission to the Creek Indians on the frontier of Georgia. There are several surprising aspects to this request: Willett's reputation for dealing with Indians was limited to the North; he had never been in the South and had no particular knowledge of the natives there. His selection could not be a political reward, since, as an anti-Federalist, he was part of the opposition. Good-naturedly, and perhaps ready for some adventure seven years after the end of the war, Willett accepted. After an arduous journey through the back country of Georgia, he reached the Creek leader, a shrewd and talented halfbreed named Alexander McGillivray.

Willett kept a journal of his expedition, in which he described participating in Indian rituals and observing their customs with the same enthusiastic curiosity he had shown in his youth. A year earlier Benjamin Lincoln had gone on a similar mission but had been rebuffed by McGillivray. In marked contrast, Willett enjoyed such complete success that McGillivray returned to New York with him. The United States, early in its first administration under the new Constitution, was spared a war for which it was poorly prepared. This outcome is not entirely a tribute to Willett or a condemnation of Lincoln. McGillivray was basically hostile to the United States and hoped to form an alliance with Spain (which still held Florida and the trans-Mississippi country). In the year between the two American initiatives Spain backed off, leaving McGillivray little choice but to come to terms with the United States.[125] In New York City the exotic McGillivray became an instant celebrity and was treated to a preliminary version of the ticker-tape parades for which the metropolis became famous.

Willett's conspicuous success brought his name to the fore when similar services were needed two years later. In April 1792 he received notification that he had been appointed a brigadier-general to serve in an army being formed to renew war against the Indians in the Ohio country, where a former officer of the War for Independence, Gen. Arthur St. Clair, had suffered a humiliating defeat. Willett would have joined the illustrious company of Anthony Wayne and Daniel Morgan, although the list was tarnished by the inclusion of the notorious Jamie Wilkinson.

At the instant when he seemed to be on the verge of receiving the recognition and position he had long craved, Willett was instead dismayed. Having gotten wind of the pending appointment, he dispatched an urgent and typically straightforward letter to his friend President Washington. In it he expressed his profound reluctance to see the United States engage in another Indian war. He went on to describe his personal feelings toward the natives, using language that to us seems somewhat generalizing and patronizing, but for its time and place was remarkably enlightened and sympathetic:

It has been my uniform opinion, that the United States ought to avoid an Indian war. . . . From my knowledge and experience of these people, I am clear that it is not a difficult thing to preserve peace with them. That there are bad men among them, and that these will at times do acts which deserve punishment, is very clear. But I hold, that to go to war, is not the proper way to punish them. Most of the Indians that I have had any knowledge of, are conceited and vain. By feeding their vanity you gain their good opinion; and this in time procures their esteem and affection. By conciliating their good will, you will render them susceptible of almost any impression. They are credulous, yet suspicious. They think a great deal; and have in general good notions of right and wrong. They frequently exhibit proofs of grateful minds; yet they are very revengeful. And though they are not free from chicanery and intrigue, yet if their vanity is properly humored, and they are dealt justly by, it is no difficult matter to come to reasonable terms with them. The intercourse I have had with these people, the treatment I have myself received from them, and which I have known others to receive, makes me an advocate for them. To fight with them, would be the last thing I should desire.[126]

Characteristically, Willett then proceeded to outline his ideas on how warfare with the Indians could be conducted. Like Benjamin Lincoln and many other Americans who grappled with this issue, Willett offered no formula to resolve the dilemma of maintaining peace with the natives while at the same time opening their lands for white settlement. It is interesting, however, that he personally did not seem to participate in grabbing Indian land. As far as is known, his extensive holdings lay east of the 1768 treaty line, and he did not benefit from the often dubious procedures by which New York acquired Iroquois lands after the war.

Taking Willett's attitude to heart, Secretary Knox responded with an offer to send him as an emissary to a peace conference at the Miami Indian villages in present Ohio. Willett again declined, this time citing his duties as sheriff at a time when "disagreeable and disorderly appearances in this city, arising from the numerous bankruptcies which have lately taken place" supposedly required his presence.[127] Not yet discouraged, Knox several months later proposed giving Willett a temporary or permanent mission among the four southern Indian nations.[128] Willett's reply does not survive, but he obviously did not accept. He thereby sacrificed his last opportunity for prominence on the national scene. Anthony Wayne, who might have been Willett's colleague, meticulously organized a new army, which won a signal victory against the Ohio Indians in August 1794.

Mary Willett, who died a year later, may have been ill at the time Willett declined his commissions, but he did not use that as an excuse. Nor did he fall back on the conventional alibi of diplomatic illness. With typical honesty he spurned his numerous advantages and limited his horizons to New York City. Colonel Willett owned a brilliant military reputation; he was acquainted with nearly everyone of consequence in the new republic; his patriotism was exemplary;

and his courage was proverbial. Knox himself acknowledged that, noting with respect to his proposed peace mission that "there would be but little personal hazard, (although that would not be a consideration with you)."[129]

It is further testimony to Willett that his services were solicited entirely on merit, as he was politically alien to the national administration. Willett deliberately turned away from these national opportunities, and in so doing he rejected a chance to serve his idol, Washington. (President Washington, if disappointed, seems to have forgiven Willett; for the two met a final time when Willett journeyed to Delaware in October 1796.) Instead, Willett remained in New York City, where his political ambitions would never be fully realized. Perhaps he did not want to risk his hard-won financial security, although Knox had offered a virtual blank check to accept the southern residency. In the end, Willett became almost a model for those proverbially provincial New Yorkers for whom the West begins beyond the Hudson.

Years of tension related to the Napoleonic Wars finally led to renewed war with Great Britain in 1812. One part of Willett probably yearned to take the field against the hated foe, but the wiser part reminded him that he was 72 years old and the father of young children. Fully aroused by the conflict, he contributed as he was able by offering advice and rallying support. However discredited his political notions might have become, his thoughts on military affairs still carried weight. In 1801, for example, Governor Clinton had appointed him to "superintend the work of erecting, enlarging and completing fortifications" in New York.[130]

Some of the colonel's unsolicited military advice was apparently not welcomed. In a letter to President James Madison in June 1813, Willett began with the rueful acknowledgement that "The reception of my former addresses are sufficient to create reluctance in again trespassing on your time."[131] Madison was only 11 years younger than Willett, so the issue was not generational. As a supporter of Burr, who had managed to antagonize both Hamilton and Jefferson, Willett was not a favorite of the Virginia Dynasty.

Willett's most memorable contribution to the war effort was a speech he made to a large crowd at City Hall Park on August 10, 1814—a time when American forces had not covered themselves in glory. Although he began by asking the audience's indulgence "for

Portrait of Marinus Willett as mayor, one of 12 painted by John Trumbull for New York's City Hall, where it still hangs. —Collection of the City of New York.

the talk of an old man," he soon showed that the fires burned with undiminished intensity. Marinus Willett was not one of those who had forgiven the British, and the speech was full of his old contempt. Probably recalling the dim, tense room at Fort Stanwix, he reminded the crowd of "what I have known and observed of the haughty, cruel, and gasconading nation that makes war against us." These, he said, were also the sentiments of Franklin and Washington: "Dr. Franklin delivered his opinions in his correspondence with Lord Howe; and those of General Washington I have had from his own lips." Few in the audience could match that; it was a compelling moment.

As few others could, Willett recalled the press-gangs of 58 years before and the cry "join or die" that had animated the citizens on the eve of the War for Independence. Most effectively, Willett provided living refutation of the belief that American militia were unequal to British regulars in combat. "I am living witness to the contrary," he proclaimed. "I have met them when their numbers were double mine; and I have routed and pursued them." What deserved pride was contained in those words! The great crowd echoed Willett's enthusiasm.[132]

Willett made a similar public appearance nearly ten years later in support of the Greeks, who were fighting for independence from the Ottoman Empire. Again harking back to the stirring days when the movement for independence arose in America, he asserted "The cause of the Greeks is undoubtedly the cause of liberty." Willett concluded by pledging to the cause 2000 acres of land. There is an element of sarcasm and grievance in this offer, since Willett did not actually own the land but had long believed that the state owed it to him for wartime service. This speech, made when Willett was 83, reveals much about his character. He was a solid citizen, a family man, a member of a conservative church and a believer in (and enforcer of) legal processes; yet in his aged veins coursed the same passionate love of liberty and resentment of unjust authority that had led him to swing a club in the streets of Manhattan and defy an armed British detachment half a century before.

* * *

In his final years Willett, an ancient father of youthful children, became truly a relic. He had lived into times in which he was uncomfortable, though he had helped make them possible. Yet there were compensations: although the colonel's age made him virtually a grandfather to his own children, he lived to see them well embarked on successful lives.

Willett's long and active life was crowned during the triumphal return of the Marquis de Lafayette to the United States in 1824. For more than a year Lafayette was greeted with an outpouring of adoration that overflowed the heart of the sentimental French nobleman. None of the thousands of Americans who shook the hand of Lafayette ever forgot the moment.

For aged Colonel Willett there could not be many years for such memories to ripen, but Lafayette's visit was a bright, mellow sunset, whose rays comforted him as twilight descended. During the war Willett had less acquaintance with Lafayette than officers who served with the main army. They had met early in 1778 when Lafayette was temporarily stationed in Albany while trying to organize a hopeless invasion of Canada. It is questionable how fluent Lafayette was in English at that time, and Willett never revealed any evidence of knowing French. Later in the year, the two officers were brought together again during the Monmouth campaign. They shared a devotion to Washington and apparently kept up a correspondence after the war.

By 1824 few of Lafayette's officer comrades were left, and to the tender-hearted Frenchman Willett, whose courage and dedication were beyond reproach, represented the youthful ardor of a heroic age. Willett was probably the oldest member of the delegation that met the distinguished visitor when he arrived in New York on August 15, 1824, and the illustrious Frenchman showed him special favor. A witness described their meeting as "extremely affectionate and touching," and added that "They embraced and kissed each other over and over again, like devoted lovers, and La Fayette talking to Colonel Willett very tenderly."[133] When the infirmities of age prevented Willett from attending public events, Lafayette visited him at Cedar Grove.

In the war, now distant, Marinus Willett had faced death unflinchingly on numerous occasions. When it called for him in extreme old age, on August 22, 1830, he was prepared. It was exactly 53 years since the gates of Fort Schuyler had swung open to receive Arnold's relief force at the end of the siege. New Yorkers forgave Willett his dubious political career and honored his deeds as a soldier in a time that already seemed impossibly gallant. Wealth still claimed its privileges, yet New York was a more democratic place than Willett had grown up in. The Erie and Champlain canals had been completed, bringing fabulous prosperity; New York was become the Empire State. The rich promise of the Mohawk Valley was being realized, as Willett had anticipated; each year memories of the bloodstained past faded, as the brave forts themselves—Fort Willett among them—settled into the forgiving earth. Marinus Willett, remnant of an already mythical age, belonged to the pantheon of heroes who had won these blessings.

Willett's body lay in state at his home for two days. In the summer heat of 1830 more than 10,000 mourners, recognizing that they had lost both a hero and a connection to a heroic age, gave homage to the savior of the Mohawk Valley. The funeral procession was so long that it reached the graveyard of Trinity Church after dark. Marinus Willett was laid to rest by the lurid flare of torches, flickering off the ruined faces of the old veterans and the smooth faces of young soldiers who were fortunate to live in a time of extended peace. It was customary in that age for church bells to toll the years of the deceased, but Colonel Willett was a military man, so his burial was marked by the booming of a minute gun fired from the Battery. Ninety times the mourners heard that heavy, insistent sound, dulled by the thick late summer air of the harbor; and in that relentless tolling they had ample time to reflect on how much they owed to Colonel Marinus Willett and the other patriots of his departing generation.

Weathering has almost effaced Marinus Willett's tombstone at Trinity Church, but a patriotic organization has erected a more durable marker nearby. Alexander Hamilton, whose political opinions were far apart from Willett's and who was slain by Willett's ally Aaron Burr, is buried a short distance away.

Acknowledgments

I am grateful for the generous assistance of many individuals and institutions who helped make this book possible. Among them are Albany County historian Virginia Bowers; George M. Clark; Craig Davis, William Lange, Susan Jones and other staff members of Fort Stanwix National Monument; Philip Lord; Glenadore Wetterau of the Fort Plain Museum; staffs of the Art Commission of the City of New York; the New-York Historical Society Reference Room; the New York Public Library Special Collections Division; and the New York State Library. Special thanks are due to Albert (Jim) Willett who shared his vast genealogical information on the Willett Family. If I have inadvertently neglected anyone, I hope they will forgive me.

ENDNOTES

Abbreviations:
MNHP—Morristown (NJ) National Historic Park
N-YHS—New-York Historical Society
NYPL—New York Public Library
NYSL—New York State Library

1. Jones, Thomas, *History of New York during the Revolutionary War*, 2 vols., edited by Edward F. DeLancey. New York: New-York Historical Soc., 1879; reprint, Arno Press, 1968, I, 215-16.

2. *A Narrative of the Military Actions of Colonel Marinus Willett, Taken Chiefly from His Own Manuscript, Prepared by His Son, William Marinus Willett.* New York: G. & C. & H. Carvill, 1831. Hereafter, *Military Actions.*

3. Ibid., 10.

4. Ibid., 11.

5. Ibid., 13.

6. Ibid., 13.

7. Frederick A. Rahmer, *Dash to Frontenac.* (Rome, NY: Published by the Author, 1973), 49.

8. Dumas Malone, ed., *Dictionary of American Biography*, XX. (New York: Scribner's, 1936), probably based on information in Benson J. Lossing, *Pictorial Field-Book of the Revolution*, 2 vols (New York: Harper & Brothers, 1860).

9. Daniel E. Wager, "Col. Marinus Willett: The Hero of the Mohawk Valley," an Address Before the Oneida Historical Society, Utica, NY, 1891.

10. Jones, *New York during the Revolutionary War*, I, 216. What could be lost, of course, was Willett's life.

11. Religious sensibilities may have influenced Willett's attitudes. His letters reveal deep religious feeling which, despite his upbringing, resembles the dissenting ideas of the Presbyterians and Puritans who were in the forefront of resistance in the northern colonies.

12. Michael Kammen, *Colonial New York*. (New York: Charles Scribner's Sons, 1975), 345.
13. *Military Actions*, 30.
14. Letter to New York State delegates in Congress; Lloyd W. Smith Collection, Morristown (NJ) MNHP.
15. Nov. 19, 1775; Willett Family Papers, NYSL.
16. Howard Thomas, *Marinus Willett*. (Prospect, NY: Prospect Books, 1954), 41-45.
17. Lossing says the British had nine killed in this encounter (*Pictorial Field-Book*, i, 741).
18. A long-running debate exists over the proper name of this fort. Although "Fort Schuyler" was used in most contemporary correspondence, it is questionable whether the renaming was official. More importantly, Fort Stanwix is the name that has endured into modern times and is used for the National Park site, so it would be unnecessarily confusing to return to Fort Schuyler. We are left with the irony that we preserve the name of a British officer instead of a dedicated American patriot.
19. The fact of the speech, however, remains beyond doubt. It was mentioned in a letter Willett wrote to Governor Trumbull of Connecticut shortly afterward (reprinted in *Military Actions* and elsewhere).
20. *Military Actions*, 57-58.
21. Ibid., 59.
22. Gansevoort Military Papers, typescript in NYSL, 159.
23. Larry Lowenthal, ed. *Days of Siege*. (Eastern Acorn Press, 1983), 50.
24. Gansevoort Military Papers, NYSL, 177.
25. Letter to New York State delegates in Congress; Lloyd W. Smith Collection, MNHP.
26. Willett to Clinton, Dec. 7, 1777; Willett Papers, N-YHS (emphasis in original).
27. Draft reply, Clinton (Poughkeepsie, NY) to Willett, Dec. 18, 1777 (on reverse of Willett letter of Dec. 7).
28. Gansevoort Military Papers, NYSL, 189.
29. "Proclamation to the chief sachems and warriors of the Oneida & Tuscarora Nations and to be forwarded by them to the Onondago sachems," Willett Papers, N-YHS.
30. *Military Actions*, 69.
31. Klock to Gov. Clinton, June 5, 1778; *Public Papers of George Clinton*, 10 vols. (Albany: New York State, 1899-1914) V, 327-29.
32. Gates (Peekskill, NY) to Henry Laurens, June 20, 1778; Gates Papers, New-York Historical Soc., microfilm reel 10.

33. Quoted in Albert James Willett, Jr., compiler, *The Willett Families of North America*, 2 vols. (Easley, SC: Southern Historical Press, 1985.)

34. Gansevoort Military Papers, NYSL, 255.

35. Willett to Gansevoort, Nov. 2, 1779; Gansevoort Military Papers; Gansevoort-Lansing Collection; Manuscripts Division; NYPL; Astor, Lenox and Tilden Foundations.

36. William Goforth to Willett, July 22, 1779; Willett Papers, N-YHS.

37. Mary Willett to Marinus, Jr., Apr. 19, 1778; Willett Family Papers, NYSL.

38. Gansevoort Military Papers, 238, 241, 243.

39. Clinton to Washington, Mar. 3, 1779; Clinton Papers IV, 612.

40. Clinton to Willett, Mar. 15, 1779; Clinton Papers IV, 635.

41. Willett to Clinton, Mar. 22, 1779. DeRoussy (probably DeRussy in the original French) had joined the Americans in Canada and remained with them under conditions of great adversity. (Francis B. Heitman, *Historical Register of Officers of the Continental Army*. (Baltimore: Genealogical Publishing, 1967). A paradox of the situation is that his dedication to the cause may have been similar to Willett's own fervor.

42. Gen. James Clinton to Gov. George Clinton, June 22, 1779; Lloyd W. Smith Collection, MNHP.

43. A recent study of this campaign is Joseph R. Fischer, *A Well-Executed Failure*. (Columbia, SC: Univ. of South Carolina Press, 1997).

44. Aug. 6, 1779; Gansevoort-Lansing Collection, NYPL.

45. Gansevoort to Caty, Aug. 6, 1779; Gansevoort-Lansing Collection, NYPL.

46. Willett to Clinton, Oct. 23, 1779; Clinton Papers V, 327-29.

47. Gansevoort to Willett, Mar. 7, 1780; Gansevoort-Lansing Collection, NYPL.

48. Willett to Gansevoort, Feb. 19, 1780; Gansevoort-Lansing Collection, NYPL.

49. Gansevoort to Willett, Dec. 18, 1779; Gansevoort-Lansing Collection, NYPL.

50. Willett ("Camp at Pumpton" [Pompton, NJ]) to Gansevoort, Nov. 15, 1779; Gansevoort-Lansing Collection, NYPL.

51. *Military Actions*, 71.

52. Allan S. Everest, *Moses Hazen and the Canadian Refugees in the American Revolution*. (Syracuse: Syracuse Univ. Press, 1976), 77-78.

53. Willett to Col. Abeel, Mar. 23, 1780; Willett Papers, N-YHS; Willett to Gansevoort, Mar. 31, 1780; Gansevoort-Lansing Collection, NYPL. In the latter, Willett refers to "the unhappy accident I met with."

54. C.P. Greenough Collection, Massachusetts Historical Society.

55. Willett's command of the regiment was not made permanent until July 1, 1780 (Heitman, *Historical Register*).

56. Willett to New York delegation, May 24, 1780; Willett Papers, N-YHS.

57. Clinton Papers VI, 216-221.

58. Washington to Willett, Oct. 24, 1780; (John C. Fitzpatrick, ed., *The Writings of George Washington from the Original Manuscript Sources 1745-1799*, 39 vols., Washington, 1931-44), 20, 254.

59. Willett to New York delegates, Lloyd W. Smith Collection, MNHP.

60. Wager, "Col. Marinus Willett."

61. Clinton to Willett, Apr. 28, 1781; Clinton Papers VI, 807.

62. Willett to Clinton, May 21, 1781; in William Ogilvie Comstock, *Four Mounted Messengers of the Revolution*. (Brookline, MA, 1913).

63. Ibid.

64. "A Return of a Regiment of levies raised for the immediate defence of the frontiers of this State Commanded by Colonel Marinus Willett," May 21, 1781; Willett Papers, N-YHS.

65. Willett to Capt. Peter Elsworth, May 19, 1781; Willett Papers, N-YHS.

66. Schuyler to Gen. James Clinton, May 24, 1781; Revolutionary War Manuscripts in the New York State Library no.1530.

67. "Regimental Orders for Colonel Willett's Regiment of Levies," May 21, 1781; Willett Family Papers, NYSL.

68. This issue is discussed in Robert B. Roberts, *New York's Forts in the Revolution*. (Rutherford, NJ: Fairleigh Dickinson Univ. Press, 1980), 383-87. Additional confusion is caused by the fact that a Fort Plank was located nearby.

69. Nelson Greene, ed., *History of the Mohawk Valley, 1614-1925*, 2 vols. (Chicago: S.J. Clarke, 1925), 1, 777. The spring of 1781 seems early for the naming, if not the construction, as Willett had only recently arrived and had not yet reestablished his reputation.

70. The approximate location of Fort Willett is known, but the site has not been precisely identified or investigated.

71. Willett to Washington, July 6, 1781; draft in Willett Papers, N-YHS. A slightly different, probably later, version is found in *Military Actions*, 73-79.

72. Willett added "I confess myself not a little disappointed in having such a trifling force for such extensive business as I have upon hand." (Willett to Clinton, July 6, 1781; draft in Willett Papers. A slightly different version is contained in *Military Actions*, 79-80.)

73. Willett to Washington, July 6, 1781 (c.f. Note 71).

74. As is typical of such encounters, reports of numbers engaged vary. In a letter to Governor Clinton reproduced in *Military Actions*, 81, Willett gives the enemy strength as 200. William L. Stone, *Border Wars of the American Revolution*, (New York: Harper & Bros., 1843), 146, places the number at 200 to 300; later writers have made it even higher. In a fragment of a draft reporting the battle to an unknown correspondent, Willett describes the enemy force as "nearly of the same number with us." (Willett Papers, N-YHS).

75. "So successful was Col. Willett in all his movements, that the Indians, believing him to be possessed of supernatural power, gave to him the name of the Devil." (William M. Campbell, *Annals of Tryon County*. New York: Baker & Scribner, 1849, 112.)

76. Willett to Clinton, July 15, 1781; Clinton Papers VII, 78.

77. Clinton to Willett, July 18, 1781; Clinton Papers VII, 90.

78. Willett to Clinton, Sep. 22, 1781; Clinton Papers VII, 350.

79. Willett to Clinton, Oct. 2, 1781; Clinton Papers VII, 370.

80. Washington to Willett, July 14, 1781; *Writings* 22, 378.

81. Willett to Clinton, Nov. 2, 1781; Clinton Papers VII, 472.

82. *War Out of Niagara*. (New York: Columbia Univ. Press, 1933), 240.

83. Willett's final report estimated that he had lost only about ten and did not attempt to estimate enemy losses (Willett to Clinton, Nov. 2, 1781; Clinton Papers VII, 474).

84. Marinus Willett certificate, Jan. 26, 1792; Willett Papers, N-YHS.

85. Willett to Clinton, Nov. 2, 1781; Clinton Papers VII, 473.

86. Swiggett discusses this issue in *War Out of Niagara*, 96-97.

87. Willett to Clinton, Nov. 2, 1781; Clinton Papers VII, 474.

88. The fact that prisoners taken earlier in the raid were brought in to Oswego suggests that most of the raiders survived.

89. Stirling to Clinton, Nov. 6, 1781; Clinton Papers VII, 479-80.

90. Willett to Clinton, Nov. 2, 1781; Clinton Papers VII, 475.

91. Willett to Clinton, Dec. 17, 1781; Clinton Papers VII, 597.

92. Willett to Clinton, Sep. 22, 1781; Clinton Papers VII, 350.

93. Petition to Willett, July 23, 1782; Willett Papers, N-YHS.

94. Another potential for confusion of names arises here: there had been an earlier fortification known as Fort Oswego; but it had been demolished, and the existing structure was the rebuilt Fort Ontario.

95. *Military Actions*, 91.

96. Washington to Willett, Jan. 23, 1783; *Writings* 26, 57.

97. Willett, Fort Herkimer, to Washington, Feb. 8, 1783; Willett Family Papers, NYSL.

98. George M. Clark, "Washington's Last Order: Capture Fort Ontario." Unpublished article. The expedition had probably reached the point at which the horses would require more food than they could haul; presumably they were sent back.

99. Willett to Washington, Dec. 22, 1782; transcript in Willett Papers, N-YHS.

100. There is considerable uncertainty about the physical condition of Fort Ontario at this time. Willett's description implies a reasonably sound structure. However Robert B. Roberts in his quite thoroughly researched *New York's Forts in the Revolution* (380) concludes "there is absolutely no evidence to support the conclusion that the British reconstructed the fort after reoccupying it." An Oswego historian, Charles M. Snyder, takes the middle ground, writing in *Oswego from Buckskin to Bustles* (Port Washington, NY: Ira J. Friedman, 1968), 26, that the British "restored the fort, and while it was not as imposing as its predecessors, it housed a small garrison. . . ."

101. *Military Actions*, 92.

102. Willett to Washington, Feb. 19, 1783; Willett Papers, N-YHS.

103. Ibid.

104. *Frontiersmen of New York*,(Albany: G. C. Riggs, 1882-83) 2, 645-47. The garrison brought in the ladders Willett had left behind. Unaware of Willett's actual intentions, they stood the ladders against the walls of the fort and found that they reached no more than two-thirds of the height of the parapet. The captive Americans also reported that two frozen men from Willett's party—presumably the same men who had been left behind—entered the fort and surrendered.

105. Washington to Willett, Mar. 5, 1783; *Writings* 26, 190.

106. Washington to Philip Schuyler, July 15, 1783, in Greene, *Mohawk Valley* 2, 1110.

107. Greene, *Mohawk Valley* 2, 1117. This is also the conclusion of N. Berton Alter, "Washington in the Mohawk Valley," (Fort Plain-Nelliston Historical Society, 1944). The itinerary of Washington's journey developed by these two historians appears to be incorrect in some particulars, based on later evidence.

108. Washington to Willett, Aug. 4, 1783; *Writings* 27, 79.

109. Washington to Willett, Aug. 17, 1783; *Writings* 27, 108; Aug. 29, 1783, 27, 121.

110. Washington to Willett, Oct. 16, 1783; *Writings*.

111. Clinton to Willett and Col. Lasher; Clinton Papers VIII, 318.

112. Nathan Schachner, *Aaron Burr*. (New York: A.S. Barnes, 1961).

113. John P. Kaminski, *George Clinton: Yeoman Politician of the New Republic*. (Madison, NY: Madison House, 1993), 108-109.

114. Willett to John Tayler, Albany, Sep. 23, 1787, NYSL.

115. E. Wilder Spaulding, *New York in the Critical Period*. (Port Washington, NY: Ira J. Friedman, 1963 [orig. 1932]), 221, 225, 269. These dedicated opponents did not fail utterly: their efforts were largely responsible for the adoption of the Bill of Rights as amendments to the Constitution.

116. *History of New York* 2, 546-55.

117. Harry Yoshpe, "The DeLancey Estate," *New York History* XVII (1936), 170-71. This relates only to the disposal of the East and West DeLancey farms and therefore may not indicate the full extent of Willett's acquisitions.

118. Henry Moscow, *The Street Book: An Encyclopedia of Manhattan's Street Names and Their Origins*. (New York: Hagstrom, 1978). Sheriff Street, which ran from Houston to Grand but no longer exists, appears on a map as early as 1797; but at that date could already have been named to honor Willett (Benjamin Taylor and John Roberts, "A New & Accurate Plan of the City of New York. . ." in Paul E. Cohen and Robert T. Augustyn, *Manhattan in Maps* [New York: Rizzoli, 117], 95). Willett Street was previously named Margaret Street.

119. Nov. 19, 1775; Willett Family Papers, NYSL.

120. 2, 491-492.

121. Simms did not include this episode in his earlier work on the subject, *The History of Schoharie County and the Border Wars* (1845).

122. June 20, 1777; Willett Family Papers, NYSL.

123. Albert J. Willett, Jr., *Willett Families*.

124. Society of the Cincinnati, *The Institution of the Society of the Cincinnati*. (New York, 1851).

125. David B. Mattern, *Benjamin Lincoln and the American Revolution*. (Columbia, SC: Univ. of South Carolina, 1995), 191-93.

126. Willett to Washington, Apr. 14, 1792; *Military Actions*, 116-17.

127. Knox to Willett, Apr. 18, 1792; Willett to Knox, Apr. 21, 1792; *Military Actions*, 119-121.

128. Knox to Willett, Nov. 22, 1792, in Comstock, *Four Mounted Messengers*.

129. Knox to Willett, Apr. 18, 1792; c.f. Note 127.

130. Appointment dated July 8, 1801 in Comstock, *Four Mounted Messengers*.

131. Willett to Madison, June 15, 1813; Willett Papers, N-YHS.

132. *Military Actions*, 149-53.

133. Wager, "Col. Marinus Willett." Wager had communicated with Col. Willett's two surviving sons, and this account probably derives directly from them.

INDEX